PARENTING STRATEGIES FOR RAISING ADHD CHILDREN

ENCOURAGE POSITIVE BEHAVIOR, TEACH SELF REGULATION, HELP THEM INCREASE THEIR FOCUS AND THRIVE IN SCHOOL

ELIZABETH N. JACOBS

© Copyright 2022 - All rights reserved.

The content contained within this book may not be reproduced, duplicated or transmitted without direct written permission from the author or the publisher.

Under no circumstances will any blame or legal responsibility be held against the publisher, or author, for any damages, reparation, or monetary loss due to the information contained within this book. Either directly or indirectly. You are responsible for your own choices, actions, and results.

Legal Notice:

This book is copyright protected. This book is only for personal use. You cannot amend, distribute, sell, use, quote or paraphrase any part, or the content within this book, without the consent of the author or publisher.

Disclaimer Notice:

Please note the information contained within this document is for educational and entertainment purposes only. All effort has been executed to present accurate, up to date, and reliable, complete information. No warranties of any kind are declared or implied. Readers acknowledge that the author is not engaging in the rendering of legal, financial, medical or professional advice. The content within this book has been derived from various sources. Please consult a licensed professional before attempting any techniques outlined in this book.

By reading this document, the reader agrees that under no circumstances is the author responsible for any losses, direct or indirect, which are incurred as a result of the use of the information contained within this document, including, but not limited to, — errors, omissions, or inaccuracies.

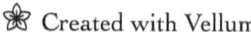 Created with Vellum

CONTENTS

Introduction   v

1. Understanding ADHD and Your Child's Frustration   1
2. They're Different, It's Beautiful   23
3. Embracing Who They Are   41
4. Remove the Obstacles   65
5. Developing New Belief Systems and Healthy Alternatives   87
6. Your Child is a Sponge   115

Final Words   125
About the Author   129
References   131

JUST FOR YOU FOR BUYING MY BOOK

A FREE GIFT TO MY READERS...

The 5 Day Challenge to Improving Communication

Anyone can implement this challenge right away and instantly start improving the relationships in their lives!

Visit the link:

Elizabethnjacobs.com

INTRODUCTION

"The diagnosis [of ADHD] made me want to prove everyone wrong. I knew that, if I collaborated with Michael, he could achieve anything he set his mind to."

— Debbie Phelps, Mother of Michael Phelps

If you're a parent, an aunt or uncle, teacher, or friend of someone with ADHD, you likely know that quote. I know the first time I read it, my heart swelled. Of course, Michael Phelps is a champion swimmer! He must have brimmed with potential as a young man. Luckily for him, his mom saw his extra energy as a blessing, not a curse. She knew the answer wasn't more sitting still but a better lifestyle for her son.

Stories like Michael's inspire me every day, and kids like him are why I wrote this book.

I have worked with kids and their families my entire life. For years, I taught at the elementary level. I found one small piece of teaching that stood out above the rest - I loved connecting with my students on an emotional level. They seemed to sense my openness and patience.

Almost daily, one of my students would open up to me about a problem they could not solve and asked for guidance. Some had parents that frightened them, and others couldn't remember the last time mom or dad spent quality time with them. But overwhelmingly, a lot of my students labeled themselves "dumb" or "stupid," and that was the reason they struggled in school.

These kids had unique brains that seemed calibrated for different functions. I sometimes got so caught up in the mechanics of how they learned that they needed to remind me to teach them! The more I dug into their beliefs that they simply couldn't understand, the more I discovered similar patterns in their learning and thinking.

While I worked daily to help these kids, something else became ingrained in them. They saw themselves as someone who needed help and wouldn't be able to do anything independently, ever. On top of that, a student who understood the math problem or could easily read what was written on the board sat right next to this poor, misguided kid, cementing that message.

As the years went on, I found I could help more kids outside of my daily lessons. Many of my colleagues agreed that I should work outside of the classroom - the kids trusted me, their parents tended to open up to me, and a lot of them asked me for advice. I already did a lot of advising for free, so why not get paid for it?

I took some psychology classes back when I studied to be a teacher, and I loved them. I felt I needed a rudimentary understanding of psychology to be an effective teacher. Furthermore, I loved learning about the brain and human behavior.

I enjoyed a university setting, but I watched many of my classmates' struggle with the work. Many found they couldn't study the massive amount of text our teachers loved to assign.

I spoke with a few of my classmates about their issues and found myself back in my old role of pro-bono-therapist.

"I can't sleep. Nothing I do turns my brain off at night."

"I take notes, but then I can't find them. I'm so disorganized!"

"I'm always late to class, even when I wake up early."

All of this played on repeat in my head as I heard my younger students get frustrated with their own tendency to misplace things or tell me they couldn't seem to get any sleep. One little boy insisted, "I just don't have a brain like the other kids!"

Though he said it in an emotional state, he tapped into the real problem. He did have a different kind of brain, and it didn't learn like everyone else. He and many of my other students, former classmates, and even some colleagues shared the same issue - ADHD.

Their issues with studying, organization, frustration, and anger at themselves spurred me to action. I spoke with professionals and read books by those who specialized in learning disorders and found that the problem went much deeper than just getting distracted regularly.

When I opened a small office in my home and started working with different children, my colleagues encouraged me to keep up to date on publications about the problem. ADHD studies constantly come out, new treatments get discovered, and as a society, we change our perspective on hyperactive kids all the time.

I continue to see symptoms of ADHD in kids and adults during our sessions. When I see someone with this different yet fascinating way of thinking, I want to dive in.

ADHD is something society has labeled a problem, but it is simply a kind of brain we don't understand. I believe kids with ADHD have endless potential, like Michael Phelps and the kids I taught back in my old school. This does not have to be an obstacle to learning. Instead, it can be a chance for you to connect with your child on a deeper and more meaningful level and hopefully learn about yourself, too.

This book will look at what ADHD is, what it does to the brain, why it's essential to accept your child as they are and not fight their nature, and how that acceptance can help them flourish.

No one can cure or get rid of ADHD, it is complex and with your growing child their ADHD grows and evolves too. I didn't write this book to make you feel like something is wrong with your child, far from it. I want you to see the beauty in your child and why their ADHD only makes them more special, not less. Let them shine, and the world will recognize your child for what they are: a superstar.

1

UNDERSTANDING ADHD AND YOUR CHILD'S FRUSTRATION

Many of the parents I have met have adverse reactions to the term ADHD. But, I often find that's because they don't know exactly what the disorder or the acronym means. They assume I mean their child is unintelligent (rarely true), high energy, or I don't want to do the hard work of behavior management and rely on medications.

After we break down the meaning of the words, the disorder as a whole, and how it works, most parents come around. Before we start, I want to make sure you know how ADHD is defined in the medical community, how it works inside the brain, and how it can make your child's life difficult.

ADHD is defined by the Center for Disease Control (CDC) as the most common neurodevelopmental disorder for children. Any kid who can't seem to stop his impulses, can't calm down, or struggles to focus can be diagnosed with ADHD. This isn't something a person outgrows - many people diagnosed with ADHD experience symptoms of the problem well into adulthood.

A kid with ADHD may display some or all of the following behaviors:

- Consistent daydreaming
- Constantly misplacing things or fidgeting
- Squirming after a few moments of sitting down
- Incessant talking
- Makes lots of careless mistakes or takes unnecessary risks
- Can't seem to resist temptation
- Struggles to take turns during play or activities
- Has a hard time getting along with others

Doctors look for one of three types of ADHD:

1. **Predominantly Inattentive Presentation -** Someone with this ADHD can't remember exact details of daily routines and gets easily distracted.
2. **Predominantly Hyperactive-Impulsive Presentation -** This is the kid who grabs things out of other children's hands, interrupts constantly, and can't stop fidgeting. These children also tend to jump, climb, and run all day.

3. **Combined Presentation** - This is any combination of the previous two types. Often the two sets of symptoms appear equally in children.

Many parents feel there's a rush to diagnose children with ADHD, but I find it's usually the opposite. Many of my teacher friends tell me about struggling students, but their parents aren't always open to discussing possible causes or solutions. They feel the issues tend to be pushed to the side, usually due to fear of the unknown.

For those diagnosed, different studies estimate that 8.4% of children have ADHD, and about 2.5% of adults struggle with it throughout their lives. It tends to be more present in boys than girls, but girls also struggle with severe ADHD.

Doctors don't know what exactly can cause ADHD, though the prevalent theory is genetics. Most people with ADHD also have a family member with the disorder. Some professionals believe the problem could also stem from premature birth, exposure to alcohol or tobacco during pregnancy, or a brain injury. But, we aren't here to dwell on the cause as it is all speculation. We want to dive into how it works within your child's brain.

ADHD and The Brain

A teenage client of mine came in fidgeting and aggravated one day. She kept pacing around my office, but I could tell it wasn't because of her ADHD. Something was on her mind.

"My friend said something today," she mumbled, still pacing.

"What did she say?" I waited a long time for the answer, but she stared straight at the floor, squeezing her hands into fists, then releasing them, then fists again.

"She said something about how my brain doesn't have the same shape, or mass, or something, like everyone else." She turned away, tears falling onto her shirt. "Is she right?"

I explained that her friend probably meant ADHD affects the brain's physical structure. I didn't think the friend said the comment as an insult, but perhaps she'd said it ineloquently. Together we looked at some images of brains in neurotypical and neuroatypical like her. We discussed the differences in more medical terms to remove the sting of thoughtless comments and give my client more power over her situation.

ADHD creates a misfire in the neurotransmitters of the brain. Instead of the brain carefully assigning tasks to different sections of the grey matter, it starts to short circuit. Kids with ADHD have low levels of a neurotransmitter called norepinephrine. This transmitter has a direct link to the brain's dopamine, or the nice, happy feeling our brain releases after a lot of physical activity or winning a game. While a neurotypical child feels a sense of accomplishment after winning a game of tag, a child with ADHD can barely register the win. The lack of dopamine sets the brain on a wonky path and makes it meander around looking for that nice, happy feeling.

The overall misfire creates issues in four different sections of the brain:

First, the frontal cortex struggles to complete high-level functions. These include paying attention, organizing time or tasks, and executive functions. Executive functions are our abilities to start a task, control our emotions, control impulses, and maintain a level of self-awareness. It also helps us adjust our behavior to new situations.

The second problem happens in the limbic system, located deep inside the base of the brain. It helps us control our emotions and pay attention for a long time.

The third is the basal ganglia. This helps us keep up with a conversation and process what we hear. The misfire in the ADHD brain makes it much harder to take in spoken or auditory information (such as in a school lesson). A misfire in the basal ganglia often leads to students acting on impulse, seemingly without any awareness of what they're doing.

Finally, there's the reticular activating system, right at the brain's core, that acts as a hallway to help messages get from one section to another. When it malfunctions, children become more hyperactive and continue to struggle to pay attention.

An ADHD brain not only functions in new ways; it also looks different from a neurotypical brain. If you look at a model brain from a neurotypical child and compare it with a child diagnosed with ADHD, you would see incredible differences. The neurotypical brain would be made of dense, grey stuff. The ADHD brain would have less grey matter. You would see shape abnormalities in the second brain, a lower volume of the overall matter, and sections within the brain that looked smaller.

These differences add up to a student who isn't getting that dopamine rush from a job well done, good grades in class, or a victory at playing tag. Instead, there's a distinct lack of joy in these tasks, and dopamine must be found elsewhere. Meanwhile, the child struggles to speak with the adults around him and can't explain how he feels. If you don't have ADHD yourself, take a moment to imagine how all of that must feel. It's no wonder, so many kids with this issue have incredible amounts of frustration.

Why is ADHD So Common Now?

People today have more access to healthcare than ever before, so we all get diagnosed with different issues more often than generations past. Those who don't have high-priced healthcare in their budget can usually visit a free clinic or talk to a professional in a public school. With our unlimited sources of information and ability to visit doctors and specialists, more people can have their child assessed for ADHD.

There's also a raised awareness of the problem. While once ADHD was seen as misbehavior, laziness, or a personality type, we now know this problem happens within the brain, and there are things that can help.

Another part of this is simply knowing the symptoms of ADHD. The same thing happens when we learn a new vocabulary word. Before anyone taught you the meaning of "ascertain," you could swear you'd never heard it before. Now that you know it, you hear it all the time. Symptoms of ADHD can have the same effect. Once you know what to look for, it's everywhere.

That said, the rate at which people are being diagnosed with ADHD is increasing. Most of this is attributed to genetics - we seem to be passing the ADHD genes around more easily. Professionals estimate the genetic factor contributes about 70 to 80% of the risk a child will have ADHD. Why is this gene more prominent now? We don't know the exact cause; only that genetics seems to play a significant role.

The remaining 20 to 30% of the risk comes from the child's environment. This includes issues at birth, such as premature birth, low birth weight, exposure to alcohol or cigarette smoke during pregnancy, or an early head injury.

. . .

Does Your Child Actually Have ADHD?

I want to take a moment and address concerns that I often hear about kids being over-medicated or having "normal kid behavior" diagnosed as a condition. Far be it from me to say that this doesn't happen.

Sometimes, a child who falls on the younger side of her grade can act immature and frustrate classmates simply because the older kids have more patience or feel more comfortable with the classroom routine. If your child's birthdate puts them on the young side for their grade, talk to your child's teacher about their specific observations.

If you feel what's happening is more age-related than not, my advice is to stay vigilant and keep observing your child. Being the little one in class can be a bigger problem for elementary students.

Another possibility is our inclusion of vague descriptions of symptoms now considered acceptable for medical professionals trying to diagnose a child. Something unacceptable in the adult world, like jumping on furniture or making loud animal noises out of nowhere, is often fine or at least normal for kids. Their desire to jump around and play instead of reading a long story isn't ADHD. It's youth.

The real issue with misdiagnosing happens when medication, labels, and a misunderstanding of a child's mental state do more harm than good. If you've ever had a doctor determine you have a problem you don't actually have, you know how this feels. It seems no matter how honest you are, no one listens. Everyone just wants to put a name to your issue and move on.

For young children, getting misdiagnosed with ADHD can create mistrust between them and the adults in their lives. It can make them hate school or authority figures, develop a fear of doctors, give them a deep sense of frustration, or create the belief that nothing they do is right. In extreme cases, it can lead to depression and fatigue.

So, do I think a lot of kids get misdiagnosed? Not really. I've met so many kids who need ADHD help only to hear their parents insist that "everyone has an attention disorder these days," or something similar. Whatever your child is going through, do your best to observe and value what you see and hear. Remember, kids often struggle to express how they're feeling and thinking.

A Deeper Look at the Signs and Symptoms

I worked with a young boy whom I knew through his teacher. He was eight years old and couldn't make it through a story without sighing, interrupting at odd moments, and fidgeting. He found the urge to run and open the classroom door too strong to resist, no matter how hard he fought it.

When we met, the boy insisted, "I love when the teacher reads to us!" yet he couldn't make it through a chapter. We talked about how he felt, and I watched as his eyes darted around the room, and he kept moving his feet no matter how much I tried to get him to relax. He managed to describe part of his favorite story, but the knick-knacks around my office demanded his attention, and quickly he was bouncing around the room.

This lack of attention twists the best intentions into a free fall of non-stop activity. My client wanted desperately to participate in class, he loved his teacher, yet nothing he did seemed to work. All his attempts to be a good, attentive student failed. This led to him getting a sharp word from his teacher because he couldn't manage to stay in the room.

But what about older kids? Many teenagers with ADHD struggle to keep track of assignments, notes, or events. Deadlines sneak up on them. Attempted assignments come back with bad grades because they don't meet the criteria, or they get forgotten in a backpack and never make it to the teacher. As kids get older, they either pick up certain tricks to help them pay attention or give up on the idea and avoid situations that demand long hours of sitting and listening.

Many kids in this older bracket have parents who advocate for them or feel comfortable telling a teacher, "I have trouble paying attention," but not all of them. I've met far too many who simply throw up their hands and insist, "I can't do it!" Frustration is the primary emotion I see in a child with ADHD. They have every intention to study hard, take good notes, and get their calendars organized. However, all their efforts fall short by the end of the week, leaving them feeling defeated.

So, what about part two - hyperactivity? Everyone lives a little more dangerously in their teen years, but hyperactivity can lead to significantly more violent and life-threatening actions. While this tendency can lead to lots of jumping and running around in children, it can mean dangerous activities with little regard to the risk for teens.

When kids reach dating age, this can present a whole new challenge for those with ADHD. They may struggle with impulse drive, which can make them do things their partner might not like or find unacceptable. Despite feeling love for a boyfriend or girlfriend, the hyperactive teen struggles to be a suitable date, much less a solid partner. An older person with hyperactivity might drive erratically or with little regard for passengers or someone trying to cross the street. An untreated case of ADHD leads to someone who gets bored fast and seems to run into trouble. Other issues can be the tendency to get into fights or impulsively look for the most dangerous situation. All of this comes with the endless frustration that nothing seems to help.

What It Means If Your Child Has ADHD

If your child gets a diagnosis of ADHD, there are several truths you need to face:

First, you'll need medical and psychological professionals in your life. This means you and your partner need to take on additional responsibilities to ensure your child gets all the help available. Talk with your pediatrician and any nearby therapist, a school counselor, family counseling center, or support group. You and your child need support through the many adjustments. Chat with any teachers or educational professionals who interact with your child during the day. Ask what resources or plans are available to you, like an Individual Education Plan (IEP), that can set benchmarks for your child and record any changes.

Second, you need to tell your son or daughter the diagnosis. Explain that they need to learn differently because their brain doesn't function the same way as most other kids, and that's okay! Kids appreciate straight talk more than anyone I know.

Then, in terms your child can understand, explain that they will have a coach in the classroom. Remind them that they need to ask for breaks when class gets too long or too difficult. Break down any new things like therapy sessions, doctor visits, or new medications that will be part of a new routine.

Finally, start working towards acceptance. Find names of accomplished people with ADHD, seek out other parents with more experience raising children with this learning disability, and stay in touch with teachers. Talk to your child about anything they feel throughout the day, when they get tired or when they can't seem to sleep so that you can give your pediatrician as much information as possible.

A client of mine came in exhausted every day from trying to get her son to do his homework, but the constant battle took a toll. When I suggested she could get him tested for ADHD, her spine stiffened.

"I don't believe in that sort of thing," she told me. I asked her why not, and she explained that if a student wanted to learn, he would. Her son's problem, she insisted, was his lack of desire to learn.

"Did he ever say to you, Mom, I don't want to learn? I don't like it?" I asked. She stayed quiet for a long time, then asked how someone might find out if a child had ADHD.

It took several more long, drawn-out talks, but eventually, that client did take her son for a test and, as I suspected, was diagnosed with ADHD. She took a break from our sessions to focus on her son and his new situation for a few weeks, but I noticed a considerable change in her composure when she came back.

"So," I said as we sat down, "you look rested!"

She explained that yes, she felt much better those days. With several changes in her son's diet and routine, he could finally sleep and stopped wandering around the house all night. She had a new system for helping him get his school work done, and the teacher had an older student who came in and sat with him during math and reading lessons to help him stay on task.

After we talked for a while, I had to ask - "Why didn't you believe in ADHD at first?"

She took a deep breath and said, "I think I felt ashamed. Like I'd done something wrong with my kid. Now, of course, I know that's not the case. And sure, some people think it is my fault, but I don't care. They don't know what a special little guy I have for a son."

Understand How Doctors Approach ADHD

Doctors have a specific view of ADHD. It's a brain problem, and therefore it requires medication. This scares off a lot of parents. They get concerned about side effects, long-term addictions, and the costs of having a medicated child. Pills can also create issues with forgotten dosages, fears of overdosing, or the chance that the medication might be abused.

I understand the concern, and I encourage clients to find a doctor both they and their child like and trust. If a doctor is going to prescribe a long-term medication to any patient, the level of trust has to be solidified between both parties. You should never feel pressured to put your child on any medication - to medicate or not to medicate is your choice, and your doctor needs to present you with all the available options.

If you do consider medications, you'll likely get to know methylphenidate. Methylphenidate comes packed in many different names like Ritalin, Concerta, Metadate, Daytrana, and Quillivant. A 2015 study was done by The British Medical Journal (The BMJ) on kids with ADHD and were medicated with methylphenidate medications. The study followed children in the classroom, teachers' reactions to kids on the medication, and any side effects caused by the dosage.

The study found that the most common side effects were changes in sleep and appetite. The doctors doing the study wrote about these changes in a jaded tone, calling them "non-serious adverse effects." I don't know about you, but if my kids stopped eating and sleeping, I'd take that seriously.

From a medical standpoint, the improved quality of life, better relationship with teachers, and higher performance in the classroom are worth fewer hours of sleep and smaller meals. But those things can send parents into a tailspin, making them feel incredibly guilty about deciding to put their children on medications.

However, the kids I've spoken to notice a significant difference while on their medication. They tell me it's much easier to keep track of what the teacher is doing, listen to their friends, and generally stay on task. Yes, the majority of them struggle to sleep, but they don't seem overly concerned. They're kids, after all.

A lot of these issues tend to be short-lived. If you find your son or daughter isn't sleeping a full eight hours, wait it out. And, in the meantime, talk to your pediatrician about your concerns. They may have some ideas of what you can do to improve sleep during this transition.

If you decide to medicate your child, make sure you discuss it with your child first, open up the lines of communication and maintain them through the process. Ask her to tell you the moment she doesn't feel well, if she starts to feel worse, and if they'd like to try again without the medication. Make sure your child knows she's never obligated to take medications for ADHD - they're an option, not a requirement.

When It's Not ADHD

Symptoms like frustration and constant distraction can feel like ADHD, but that doesn't mean your child has a learning disability.

Angry Outbursts

One of my clients felt confident her son had ADHD. "He gets so frustrated with his reading homework. He sometimes throws his books across the room!" his mom told me. I interviewed both her and her son (let's call him David) about how they both felt.

Mom believed David could easily do his homework if he could just calm down and enjoy the story assigned to him. David felt vast amounts of pressure to read, didn't care for the topics his teacher picked out, and felt no one listened when he suggested reading other things.

We started working with David and his anger by helping him recognize it in himself. "David," I told him, "I can see you making a fist and scrunching your eyebrows together. It looks like you're getting upset. Can you tell me how you feel right now?"

I made sure to help his mother do the same, in place of commands like, "Don't get so mad!" which, predictably, only made David angrier. Helping him see what anger looked like on his face and in his body allowed him to start managing it.

David told me how much he loved to read about his favorite sports stars, so his mother and I contacted the school to ask if he might get an alternative to the usual fiction books. The teachers loved our proactive approach and immediately agreed.

We also worked with David on breathing exercises, counting down from ten, taking a moment to himself to center his emotions and keep from lashing out. In our visits, David and I talked about the importance of finding friends who know how to relax and have fun, not people who yell and throw things.

It took time, but David eventually got his anger under control. He felt seen by his family, his teacher, and his mom learned to communicate with him so the two of them would fight less. Today they're feeling much better about their relationship, and no, David does not have ADHD.

Pressures and distractions

Remember that today's kids are under constant pressure to not only fill every moment of every day, they're also expected to multitask at every moment. All of this happens under the continual lens of society; kids often have pictures of them taken and posted with or without their permission.

All of this adds up to a distracted, stressed-out kid. You can forbid phones and social media, but what happens when they need them for a class project? What will they do in an emergency or when they want to call grandma and grandpa?

It's too hard to banish these things from our lives, so I recommend working on ways to control them. For example, some apps limit what shows up on a Facebook feed, reducing the main page to posting an update or an inspiring quote. The rest of the platform is still there but isn't thrown in your face. Other options are ad blockers and alternative browsers that limit the onslaught of images, information and keep others from tracking your online behavior.

It's also important to let your kid get bored. Instead of handing over a phone or tablet, encourage your child to feel bored for thirty minutes. Boredom can help calm a child's mind, encourages creativity, and gets their temperament evened out.

A parent I work with limits access to chargers for her kids. She explains they can use their phones anytime they want, but chargers are only available twice a week. That forces her sons and daughter to think about what they do on their phones (simple messages or lots of time playing games). Knowing a charge is a couple of days away encourages her kids to manage their screen time, a valuable skill they'll have for years to come.

Remember, if you limit your child's charging time, you'll need to limit your own. Don't expect your children to respect this new rule if you refuse to follow it yourself.

More Than Anything, Kids Want to Feel Valued and Appreciated

As kids get older and navigate first loves, high school, the pressures of grades, and graduating, they start to wonder if they measure up.

It breaks my heart to hear some of my teen clients tell me about themselves. "I'm ugly. Everyone tells me I am," they'll say in a session or insist that "nothing is interesting about me." Teenagers, and sometimes young children, often identify as what they aren't. A teenage boy might think to himself, "I'm not a star football player, I don't have anyone who wants to date me, I'm not popular... no wonder my parents don't care what I do."

Kids are often shocked to hear that parents love everything about them. It's not because this hasn't been said before, but rather the lack of action moms or dads take to show their kids how much they're loved.

Here are a few things you can do to reinforce a sense of family, love, and trust in your kids.

- **Set aside time** - Make a section of your evening, or one day a week, that's just for you and your child. If you have more than one kid, separate them and spend time with them one-on-one doing something they enjoy. One kid might love a puzzle with you, while another wants nothing more than to ride a bike with you in the evening. When your kids see you consistently make time for them, they'll feel much better about themselves as people.
- **Start conversations with them** - Experiment with a few different times of day and locations for each of your kids where you can sit and listen to what they have to say. It can be about anything that's on their mind. The important thing is to show them that they have your

attention when they speak to you and that you're interested in them as a person.
- **Make clear boundaries** - Resist the urge to be the buddy parent. Set clear limits on what's allowed and reinforce those rules in your speech and actions whenever possible.
- **Be consistent** - Kids learn about us by observing our behavior. Constantly changing how you handle different situations creates a lack of trust between you and your child. A more predictable life can help your child feel safer and more in control.

All of this can help you see your child as unique, not a potential case for ADHD or another disability. Of course, I would tell a parent with an ADHD child to do all the same things, but it never hurts to get a refresher course.

Chapter Summary

Now you have a baseline for ADHD, what it looks like, and how to see the differences in a learning disability and more common problems.

- ADHD has three major presentations: Inattentive, Hyperactive-Compulsive, or Combined
- The brain of a child with ADHD looks and

functions differently from a neurotypical child's brain.
- High-stress levels, depression, and high amounts of pressure can cause neurotypical kids to have some of the symptoms of ADHD.

2

THEY'RE DIFFERENT, IT'S BEAUTIFUL

A big part of parenting a child with ADHD is acceptance, even celebration, of your child's differences. You need to see your son or daughter as someone who has all the potential, love, and creativity of any other child, yet the ability to express it in a new and exciting way.

All children need to feel secure as individuals, but life often gets in the way. As parents, we tend to project our own needs and wants onto our kids. Then we can miss the signs that we're overstepping, making our children feel guilty for not meeting our expectations or their loneliness. After all, we're not seeing the real them.

Instead of focusing on our relationship with our children, we tend to focus on behavior. This isn't entirely off-base, and it's essential to know if your kid is acting out because they are stressed over grades. But, it's easy to forget the relationship behind the behavior.

Where is Your Child Coming From?

It's essential to start thinking of your child from day one. Even if your kid is 17 years old and talking about college, try to remember what they were like as a baby. How did they respond to light, sound, touch, and interactions?

Those early signals showcased elements of the same personality you can see today. You might get frustrated with your child's messiness or refusal to play board games with the family, but have you done any digging into the why behind the choice?

Take a lack of cleaning. I work with lots of kids whose parents are appalled at the sight of their child's room. One mother came to me in a state, insisting, "I can't find another piece of pizza tacked to the wall. I cannot!" I know it's gross and needs addressing, but we can learn a lot when we can take a step back and investigate why kids do these things.

I encouraged the pizza-on-the-wall mom to have her son come in so I could evaluate him for any signs of depression. Sure enough, he was intensely depressed. It seems odd, but the gross decor was a desperate call for help. That same boy put garbage bags over the windows and sat for hours in bed, staring at the wall. His depression made it impossible for him to do anything productive, so instead, he made messes.

What about a refusal to spend time with the family? As always, we can dig a little deeper. At first, a rejection of family time can feel normal. Parents are old and lame; ask any teenager, so it doesn't feel too scary when they choose their friends over family time. But it is worth checking to see if something deeper is going on.

Is it possible your son or daughter doesn't feel heard when he or she suggests an activity? Do they feel the activities are dictated to them, making them more parent time than family time?

Try asking your child what they would like to do for fun. They may just want to pick a movie or go to a local event run by their friends. Maybe they have something in their lives that plays a much more significant role than you realized, like a custom website, a band, or an organization. Try to get involved and let your child take the reins to show how much you respect what they do, and then you'll get more respect in return.

Going Beyond Medication

In order to see your child as a whole individual, it's essential to change the way you think about them.

First, you need to put things into perspective. If your child finishes their homework and does a couple of chores before zipping out the door, that's a win. Remember, kids with ADHD have a low executive function, which makes completing a task incredibly difficult. That means any dish that gets washed and put away, any time toys end up in their proper place, or a math problem gets solved, it's time to give your little one a congratulatory hug.

Second, forget about any kind of perfectionism. Life with an ADHD child is far from perfect, so don't ever demand high, unachievable performance levels. Instead, calibrate your expectations. Will they be able to get out the door in time for school, fully dressed and homework in hand, in twenty minutes? If not, change the time to thirty or forty and adjust your morning routine.

Next, you need to communicate openly with the other people in your family. Stay transparent about the realities of ADHD and how they'll continue to affect your son or daughter in the coming years. Apologize for any time you lost your temper. Discuss your commitment to managing your stress better. Ask your other children for help and reach out to any support groups or professionals in your area who can give you more insight into your child's ADHD.

It's important to acknowledge how one child's ADHD affects other children or people in your home. Explain that you're in a time of transition and ask them for their help and patience. Let them know that you see their frustration and hear them out when they get upset or fed up.

Managing ADHD takes time and practice, but I have some excellent starting tips and tricks for you. Here's a comprehensive list of things you can do at home to help your child feel more in control of his impulses.

- Structure everything - Make sure everything in your child's day stays as predictable as possible.
- Visible clocks and timers - Use timers for everything; time in the bathroom, homework sessions, playing outside, anything you can think of that could use a time limit.
- Minimize extracurriculars - Pick one fun activity to do after school or on the weekends and resist the urge to load up your child's schedule. If your child asks to do a secondary activity, consider canceling the first one.
- Create a quiet space - Make sure your child has a neutral space (not anywhere you use for time outs) to sit quietly and be alone. Be sure to treat this as their own private time and don't interrupt or pull them away for at least 15 minutes.
- Focus on neatness and organization - The sight of a neat, organized home can help children manage their thoughts and stay calm. It will also help you if you come home to a pleasant, tidy environment.

As you work to manage your child's ADHD, you'll notice a few things that help and others that don't. Some helpful things to work on include:

- Regular bedtimes (even when meds make it challenging).
- Encouraging exercise. Get running or biking with your child whenever you can to model the habit.
- Limited screen time. Constant computer, phone, or TV viewing can enhance ADHD-based actions.
- Encourage your child to think out loud. This is a new habit meant to replace impulsive actions. It gives your son or daughter a moment to think before doing.
- Practice pausing. Before writing down an answer to a homework question, flipping the channel to a new show, or running out the door, encourage your child to stop and count to five.
- Find counseling and care for yourself. I mentioned this earlier, but I can't stress enough how important your alone time becomes when a child needs all of your attention and energy. Even if the most you can manage is a long walk on your own once a week, take it.
- Prioritize green spaces. I know not everyone lives in a place with lots of trees and grass, so do what you can. Time outside with the sky, trees, small animals, and lots of green helps ADHD kids calm down, manage their emotions, and sleep better.

With your go-to helpful things in mind, I want to encourage you to avoid one big, bad thing. Do your best to avoid negativity. Don't think negative thoughts about yourself as a parent, your child as a person, or get bogged down in bad thoughts about school or fights at home. Negativity only hurts your journey towards the acceptance of ADHD.

Short-Tempered Children

Many of the same behavior management we use with ADHD can help kids who express their anger in an unhealthy manner (bursting into screams, kicking, or hitting).

I see a lot of parents who simply need better management techniques with their son or daughter. They don't want anyone on the playground to get hit or bitten. They want fewer public outbursts and a better sense of what their child needs. One parent told me, "I just need him to take a breath and calm down!"

There are a few things to remember when kids get overly angry:

- Encourage them to pause. If a child demands a trip to the park, don't say no right away. Instead, say something to put off the discussion like, "I know you love the park. Let's think about it, okay?" Then, circle back and mention how much

you appreciate her patience. "You were so patient while I did the dishes! Now I have time to go to the park."
- Name the emotion. Phrases like "I can see that you're angry about this. Can you tell me what's going on?" are a game-changer.
- Ask your child to use her words. Start with the words, "I'm angry." After they get into the habit of expressing what they feel in the moment, you can start to add more. "I'm feeling angry that I can't have any dessert. I'm still hungry." That way, her communication grows as your kids get older.
- Forget the adage to let them cry it out. When your child goes into a full tantrum, pick them up in an authoritative manner and say, "We're going to have a talk," then sit and work it out. That teaches a child more positive techniques for controlling emotions instead of letting emotions take the reins.
- Set a solid limit about anger and actions. Emotions can't ever be the enemy - oppressed anger can lead to numerous health problems. Instead, set a limit. Be clear with your child that anger or sadness is okay. It's never okay to hit, bite, or verbally attack someone when they don't feel happy. They need to come and talk to you, write in their journal, or play basketball for a few minutes - whatever helps them work through emotions.

The critical thing to remember is that kids don't talk about emotions naturally. If they see you panic, they'll panic. If they hear you yelling, they'll do the same. Try to model things like taking a deep breath, exercising to release tension, and talking about how you feel.

A Quick Word About Tantrums

Tantrums can feel like a child's misguided attempt to control the adults in his life, but that's rarely the case. In reality, a lot of kids benefit from a good cry.

I saw a young, tantrum-prone child for several months after her mother begged me to help. I didn't really see the issue with a small child crying. At our first visit, I saw how much the mom pleaded with the little girl to stop, making the situation much tenser with her unease.

It occurred to me that two things happened with each fit. First, the little girl felt frustrated or sad about a particular problem. Secondly, she cried more when she saw how bad her tears made her mother feel. So, I made a video.

I showed the little girl attempting to draw a house in the video, then putting down her crayon and sobbing when the house didn't turn out right. I sat next to her, put a hand on her back, and gently encouraged her to try again once she was done crying. Sure enough, once she finished crying, she picked up the crayon and drew again, this time making a house to her satisfaction. When her mother saw it, her jaw dropped. It never occurred to her that crying was part of her daughter learning how to exist in the world.

Here are some other things tantrums do for children:

- It helps them work through the pain and feel better. Deborah McNamara, Ph.D., famously said, "Crying is not the hurt, but the process of becoming unhurt."
- They promote better sleep. Avoiding our feelings is a great way to ruin a night's sleep, and no one knows that more than a toddler. Working out all that stress means they'll rest well.
- It's a show of limitations, and that's good. Saying "no" and standing by your decision will upset your child, but that's okay! Help them express how they feel and work on their communication instead of avoiding the tears altogether.
- They help behavior in the long term. Avoiding a tantrum is only a means of sidestepping the symptom, not the problem. Children who don't cry it out might act out at daycare or find other ways to process their feelings. This can get in the way of their natural emotional growth.
- Tantrums are an honest expression of emotion. As we get older, we stop crying because it's less socially acceptable, but all humans want to cry and scream no matter their age. Let your child cry and howl while they can still get away with it.
- You can help your child have tantrums at home

instead of in public. Talk to your child about why home is a better place to feel strong emotions. That's where everyone has their toys, personal space, and parents to listen to them.
- Tantrums can help children and parents connect. Try to see tantrums as your chance to empathize with your child's struggles, not a standoff between the two of you.
- Keep in mind that you want your child to tell you how they feel. A tantrum is your child's way of saying, "I feel safe letting you see me at my worst."
- Tantrums kick up big emotions in parents, so pay attention to how you feel. Let your child's tantrums be a reminder to let your feelings out, to care for yourself, and to have a good cry or laugh.

Let's take a break from big, emotional moments and focus on hyperactivity for a moment. The other type of outburst many kids with ADHD have is intense, non-stop energy. This keeps them from doing what they want, derails them like a high-speed train, and often gets them hurt or in trouble.

Hyperactivity isn't necessarily a bad thing on its own. A hyperactive mind can be great. The problem we run into is when it prevents us from living the life we want. So, how can we work with hyperactivity instead of against it?

• • •

A Closer Look at Hyperactivity

Many kids with ADHD have things that hold their interest for a long time. Your child might love a particular movie and have all the words and songs in it memorized. Whatever holds his attention, you can see firsthand that the problem isn't an inability to focus but difficulty controlling where their focus lands.

Elementary school often frustrates students because they feel dragged from one subject to another. Sometimes those subjects feel like they warrant more time, which is where the frustration comes in. But our curriculums demand that students pack everything into their day, causing the kids to do an attention switch. It's something we stop doing once we go to college or the workforce, so we forget how exhausting that constant switching feels.

This idea, the lack of attention, is actually an abundance of attention that's simply misguided. One way to think of our focus is to imagine a flashlight and where you choose to point it. Your flashlight's beam might be broad, narrow, bright, or dim. You have the choice to point it down at the ground or swing it in every direction, but the hand is the boss. It makes the decision. ADHD makes the hand harder to control or takes it away altogether, meaning everything on the path or in the room gets a moment of illumination.

So, if ADHD children have a flashlight that wants to see everything, it's not necessarily a lack of attention but an excess of attention. What they need is help controlling the hand or help to manage their tendency to take in everything.

A great way to get kids more in tune with what helps them focus and what doesn't is to get them into activities and sports that require a combination of mental and physical agility. Many kids I know with ADHD play soccer or basketball; both need them to think strategically while racing across the court or field. That helps their hyperfocus kick in and helps them practice focusing on one activity at a time.

Team sports are great but encourage individual activities too. Try having your child work with her hands doing arts or crafts. One of my clients arrives with a new page of her comic every session and wants to go over it with me frame by frame. Seeing me respond to her creative work helps reinforce the idea that she can focus if she approaches an activity the right way.

One of the worst things for a child with ADHD is excessive screen time. Computers, video games, movies, and TV will get their attention, but they can lead to poor sleep and a backlog of hyperactivity. Instead of using downtime as a reason for your son to watch TV, give him a list of chores to do or activities to try.

I recommend a straightforward reward system to keep your child motivated. Make a simple one-week calendar with a chore for each day. If it gets completed, your kid gets a star. Five stars equal a new toy, a trip to her favorite place, or anything she loves but doesn't always get.

When Your Child Doesn't Fit In

A big part of being a kid with ADHD is struggling to fit in or coming to terms that they may never fit in. Their brains simply function differently, and that's not their fault.

Small children yearn for social connections, so a struggle to make friends can feel particularly painful to them. Many of my younger clients plan out long, detailed strategies they've dreamed up to help them have the most friends possible. When I suggest that having a core group of true friends is better than having everyone like them, they balk at the idea.

There's a real possibility your child will run into some social obstacles or struggle to make friends. That's okay; most children do. The critical thing to remember is that your child will look to you for your reaction and guidance on getting through difficult times.

Whenever your child expresses a desire to make a new friend, get involved in the process, then step back. It's essential to see your kid out with some pals who truly understand him and like him. Pay attention to how the group acts together and make sure you're comfortable with the dynamic. Then, when it feels right, let your child make the decisions about his social life.

Be there when he and his friends fight, but resist the urge to take charge. If your child's differences come up, listen to what he has to say about the conversation, the comments made, all of it, then help him talk about how he feels. He might get hurt, but he'll get through it.

Hyperactivity and Everyday Life

Being a hyperactive person isn't always a bad thing. Parents can do a lot to help a boy or girl celebrate being different and learn how to use it to their advantage.

First, it's a great way to teach consistency. Schedules, checklists, and highly structured days all help children with ADHD. Start with the doctor appointments. Mark all the days on a shared family calendar and talk about your child's schedule with her. Let her know that she'll always see the doctor on the fifteenth of the month, then be as consistent as possible. From there, move on to consistency in other things like mealtimes, breaks from homework, time spent outdoors, anything that can be scheduled.

Kids with ADHD struggle to sit and focus. Their bodies demand movement, so rather than fight it, just send your child out so she can run for a few minutes. Yoga breaks are effective, as are coloring, singing, and dancing. Time homework sessions and breaks, and set an alarm to go off as each finish.

When you do this, you are incorporating a method called shaping. That means you reward the behavior you want while extending it for longer each time. For instance, do five minutes of homework, then a ten-minute break for a week. The following week, extend homework to six minutes but keep break time the same. Eventually, work up to equal homework and break times, then assess if you can scale back breaks or if they need to stay as-is. Check-in with your kid as you go. Make sure she feels good about the process and understands. Try to schedule a big, explosive play session before a calm, quiet study time (with a fidget toy close by). Make sure your child understands why you're doing things a certain way.

Offer up a fidget toy for study time. A bike desk or walking desk may help as well, but most of the ADHD kids I know love to squeeze or roll something when they need to think. They also feel better if they take some time to play after school instead of jumping into homework.

Breathing exercises, meditation, and reading times in a quiet space can require some training, but they're incredibly beneficial to kids with ADHD. As a family, look for meditations, visualization exercises, writing reflections, or art therapy that your child responds to, then do it with her. She'll be more likely to build a habit if she sees the people around her doing it and reaping the benefits.

Help Your Child Love Themself

All children need expressions of love, particularly kids with ADHD who are getting negative messages from others. If teachers, classmates, or friends say things to your child that hurt his feelings or make him doubt himself, try some extra love at home.

Small kids need extra cuddles and hugs to feel better. Don't be shy with big bear hugs at the end of the day or a snuggly reading session. Build a fort together to get some peace, and then talk about how you're feeling. Remember, if you share, your kid will share.

Encourage a lot of resilience by talking about trying again, falling, and getting back up, or anything that helps your kid give it another go. If a friend is mean at school, encourage him to talk to other people. Remind him that if he made one friend, that means he can make another. If he tries and fails, be there to help with round two.

Recognize large amounts of effort. If your child feels terrified to sing with the school choir but goes through with it, verbalize how great it is to see him push through doubt. "I know you weren't sure about being in the show, but you were so brave up there!" Remember that even distracted, hyperactive kids need lots of tender loving care. That's the best thing any parent can give.

Chapter Summary

Some quick basics to remember for kids with ADHD:

- Structure and schedules are everything. Even keeping a clean house can help your child feel calm.
- Remember to schedule lots of exercise and playtime throughout the day.
- Give your child hugs, cuddles, and one-on-one time. Remind your kid that they are loved no matter what.

3

EMBRACING WHO THEY ARE

I talked to a couple of parents whose daughters had ADHD, and both told me they had days they just wished they didn't know. "It's strange," one mom said to me. "It's like, a part of me wants not to know what ADHD is or what it looks like. As if ignorance would somehow make all of this easier."

I understand. When we are forced to face a difficult reality, it's easy to miss the days before all the new stuff happened. When the house could stay dirty, the day didn't have to be so rigid, and we just didn't have to think about the tough stuff non-stop.

So, how can we get past the difficult period of wishing it would all go away and shift into full, loving acceptance? And how can we help our kids feel good about who they are, learning disabilities and all?

· · ·

Are You Forcing or Helping?

Many parents I see worry their children don't do enough. Not enough music lessons, theater group, soccer practice, you name it. We live in a time of access. I bet if you do some digging, you'll even find free options like programs available in public schools or community centers.

But, at what point are we forcing kids to do something instead of being helpful? And how can we tell what's helpful and what's hurtful when our child has ADHD? Distracted and hyperactive kids give us a unique window into how kids view the world's options. They see everything as exciting, but that excitement burns out fast. For kids with ADHD, that excitement can last as little as a few minutes, maybe a day if we're lucky.

It's essential to make peace with the idea that your child might hate something that's generally accepted as "good" for kids. I know a lot of parents who feel terrible that their child hates team sports or that a daughter stops playing the violin. Honestly, I'm finding that these decisions not to join or quit don't have long-lasting adverse effects. What drives everyone into an early grave is forcing a kid to do something he hates. I see the same pattern over and over. A parent meets another parent on their way to their child's French horn practice or painting class. The busy parent praises this incredible pastime to the parent with nothing on the calendar.

"Oh, we love it!" the parent says. "Painting class helps with socialization, spatial reasoning, and creative expression. We think little Johnny could be an artist or designer one day! You really ought to sign up!"

Sounds good, right? Sometimes, these extra activities sound so good we don't check in with our children in a way that lets us know if they'll truly enjoy this new class, sport, or past-time. The key is patience. Your son might want to join Johnny in painting class, but even so, there's no rush.

If something sounds exciting and your child has room in his schedule, talk about it first. Let him know how his schedule could change if he signs up, who will be there, and what kinds of activities he'll do in class. Then, sleep on it. The following day, see if he's still interested, then ask if your child can have a trial class. That gives you the space to try out this new, supposedly fantastic activity. Is it worth the extra driving, the money, the stress, or is it just another thing?

Again, make sure you're helping, not forcing. There's no law that says your kid needs to be creative, athletic, or academically gifted. Focus on helping him find his true self instead of creating some new, improved version of your child.

Practice Patience

Think of your patience like a muscle; it needs to be stretched and strengthened just like a bicep. You need to pay attention to your style of patience and give it a workout whenever you can. A great thing to practice is to stop, look and listen. Here's what I mean:

Imagine your daughter is running all over the couch, jumping onto the ottoman, tap dancing on the coffee table, and screaming at her highest volume. Most parents will naturally yell, "Stop! Get down! What are you doing?"

While this reaction is fair and expected, it's not patient. I don't want you to let your daughter fall and injure herself; instead, use these moments to see how patiently you can respond.

Stop - As soon as you feel the urge to yell at your child, hold back. Take a deep breath and remind yourself that if you yell, she yells. If you panic at the sight of someone doing something unexpected, she will, too. Count to five before you say anything.

Look - Take in the scene as you count. What is she actually doing? Is she destroying the furniture, breaking things, kicking valuables? Or is she playing? Why the dance on the coffee table? Is she mimicking something she saw in a movie? Get a quick visual assessment as you move in to get her down and calm.

Listen - Get your daughter down and sit her next to you. Give her a fidget toy or space to fidget, then ask, "What are you doing right now?" If she responds, "I'm playing!" then you'll know it's time to go outside and burn off some energy. But, if she says, "I'm the dancing cat from Oliver," you'll know she's copying a scene or maybe something a friend showed her. Go outside together and play or have her show you the dance and let her get all that hyperactivity out. Then, after she's calmer, talk about why you need her to play off the furniture for her safety.

By listening to her and respecting her needs, you do something incredibly powerful - you model how to be a kind, patient person. Remember, kids don't do what we say; they watch us to copy our actions. How we treat others is a massive part of that, so don't miss these opportunities to show your child how to be respectful first and foremost.

Stay Grounded and Centered

Patience is the beginning of a long, complex journey but also one that will help you reap endless benefits. You'll see changes in your child, but I can guarantee you'll see changes in yourself as well. My clients who work on their own internal peace feel much more confident about their parenting skills. They sleep deeply and peacefully and have good mental tools to help them through the bad times.

Get your negative reactions under control - Once everyone is safe and on to a new, hopefully, better activity, grab a few seconds to take stock of your emotional state. Are you thinking your child is a spoiled brat and wondering how she ended up that way? Maybe wishing she could go to Grandma's for a couple of days so you could clear your head?

These thoughts are unavoidable, but what we do with them is up to us. We can let them fester or process them and get them out.

One of my clients keeps emergency journals around the house. Her kids are still small, so she stashes them high up on bookshelves or in the kitchen and always with a nearby pen. Whenever she has a negative thought about her children, she grabs the nearest one and scribbles all those horrible things in big, ugly letters. That expels them from her head and gives her a chance to put those evil thoughts on a literal shelf, then walk away from them.

Other clients of mine swear by meditation. Meditation is an excellent tool for mood control and peace of mind. Also, it only takes a few minutes a day. Aim for a quick, five-minute meditation to start. You can find tons of free meditation videos and podcasts to help. Then, if you have the space in your day, you can gradually build up to ten or fifteen-minute sessions.

Other clarifying practices include breathing exercises or repeating a mantra. Try saying to yourself, "My child is acting like a child because she is a child," or something similar. It helps shift your perspective and keep you on track as a parent.

Set a limit - Whenever a new problem presents itself, it's time to set a limit. Remember, boundaries remind children that you're in charge and keeping them safe, so don't hesitate to create a new one that you may not have needed in the past.

This happens in three steps. First, empathize with a statement like, "You look like you are having a blast."

Second, state the issue. Explain the problem in a simple, straightforward language such as, "but yelling is too loud for inside the house. Mom is working right now, and I need a quiet place to focus and finish for the day.

Third, state what's allowed. "Why don't you go play this game outside in the front yard? I'll come to get you in twenty minutes, and we'll have a snack." It helps if you involve yourself in some way, like joining in the game for a few minutes (feel free to bring a timer), or by helping your child transition into the next thing, like snack or movie time.

ADHD kids respond much better to limits when they involve a set time. As kids get older, you can add comments like, "Feel free to hang out with your friends until four o'clock this afternoon, then we need to do an hour of homework."

Those precise, structured times help your child feel confident she knows what to do and when to do it.

Let Them Learn at Their Own Pace

I work with a few homeschooled kids, and all of them tell me that other kids expect them to be freaks of nature. Kids who attend standard school expect any child learning at home to struggle with the idea of doing things socially or that they'll be so religious they can't manage a trip to the movies or a party.

"They always ask me if I know what something is. Do you know what a latte is? Do you know what a computer is?" one boy told me. "They think just because they attend public school; they're somehow more aware of the world than I am. I'm so tired of it."

I hear many of the same concerns from parents considering letting their child do an alternative or home-based program. Will my kid be able to pass a test? Get a diploma? Make friends?

Parents of children with ADHD especially worry about pulling a child out of school. Granted, it's not always the right decision, but I have noticed something. Kids who feel free to learn at their own pace, particularly ADHD kids, thrive in a program that doesn't throw them into a cookie-cutter mold of what learning and growing are supposed to look like.

Computer genius Bill Gates publicly stated that he's found, in his independent studies, that children who don't feel pressured to meet learning deadlines and fall in line with testing expectations do much better in reading and math. Rather than approaching learning from a negative mindset of "I'm not good at this subject, so I have to work to fix the problem," they know they can be bad at something for a while.

Maybe a kid who loves to read but struggles with math focuses more on reading and less on numbers. Sure, the math comes slower, but so what? Reading is the foundation for lifelong skills, and we should celebrate a love of reading, not work to fix it.

Creativity can also be nurtured and valued outside of a standard school system. There's no award or special mark given to kids who demonstrate creative thinking and problem-solving in your average public school. It doesn't lend itself to multiple-choice questions, so most school districts don't push kids to be creative but rather to be right. That's a metric school can measure in no time.

If you feel the traditional school environment isn't going to work for your kid, look for something else. Look into private tutors, an alternative program, or homeschooling. Talk to your son and ask how he's feeling in the classroom, check in with his teacher, do anything you can to get a comprehensive view of where your child struggles and where he thrives. Then, discuss as a family how everyone does things in their own time, and that's wonderful. If the topic of home or alternative school comes up, decide how you'll proceed as a family.

Whatever you do, try to give your child time to learn on his own. Tell him you want him to celebrate what he's good at and learn the rest in a way that serves him best.

Passion-Based Learning

With so much knowledge and factual information available online, many schools are looking at what they teach and why. Do we need kids memorizing historical facts, or is it better to help them find which sites are better sources of historical narratives? Do they really need to know calculus, or is their time better spent learning graphic design and coding?

Some schools are turning to a passion-based model. Passion-based learning is what it sounds like - a school day centered around what kids love to do instead of what a test says they need to know. Remember, education norms change slowly, so even when parents and teachers agree the current model is antiquated, it won't be out of our lives for the next ten or twenty years. Even then, the changes will be minimal.

I'm not being cynical-I worked in the school system for years. I've heard all the griping in the teacher's lounge about how no one cares about authentic learning, about students' talents that get pushed aside for more time to study for tests or prepare for majors their parents chose for them. We like to think these problems are long gone, but the truth is they're ever-present.

The pain of being hammered into a mold stays with us for a lifetime and leads to indifference in education for the next generation, a hatred of teachers, and a general sense of "Well, what can we do?" A lot. We can do a lot. We live in an age where information is everywhere, new educational programs and different kinds of schools pop up every day, and we have options. Don't shrug it all off. Take advantage.

Again, bring your kid into the conversation. Tell him how following his passions and not worrying about the status quo means a better life for him. Encourage him to follow whatever passion he has at the moment, even if that fire goes out the next day. It doesn't matter. When you allow your child to dig into his interests for as long as they interest him, a few things happen.

Learning with real passion means a more focused child, which results in less lousy behavior to manage. It also means your child gets to feel a rush of dopamine that only comes with deep, genuine interest paired with the joy of discovery. Multiple interests can work in your favor as well. Kids who pursue two or three interests at once start to understand and find themselves in a more organic way than kids who feel pressured to study violin or excel at karate.

Even if your kid loves rolling in the mud, let him do it. Maybe he'll design muddy obstacle courses for people to run through or cars designed for wet environments. Who knows? It doesn't matter. It is essential to acknowledge that he loves it and respect his time in the puddles.

This Won't Happen Right Away

Every parent who loves and adores their children fall into the pit of comparison and despair, the tendency to look at other kids and wonder why our sons and daughters don't look or act the same way. It's normal. We live in a society where we all work to fit in, so don't beat yourself up for wanting your kid to be or look a certain way.

I always encourage my clients to work towards complete, radical acceptance of their children the way they are and to avoid chiseling away at kids to make them a particular kind of person. This can be tough, but it's a beautiful goal to work towards and one your child will thank you for in the long run.

How can we start working on accepting our kids? You can take a few basic steps at home to get started.

1. **Start by accepting yourself -** We tend to criticize other people more when we're not happy with ourselves. Try to see yourself for who you are, not who you wish you could be. It might help to get off social media, journal, or meditate and just spend some time with yourself. Schedule a mental health day and take some time to only do things you know feel good mentally and

physically, then take stock of the choices you made.

2. **Educate yourself -** Buy a couple of books about early childhood development, so you know what to expect in your child. The different phases of growing up can be incredibly confusing from the adult perspective, so give yourself a chance to learn the neurology of a little one's brain and how it's changing. Be sure to learn more about the ADHD brain, too, and how it differs from a neurotypical brain.

3. **Learn your child's personality -** The building blocks of your child's personality will likely be clear early on in her life. Try to see what makes her happy or excited and what brings her down. Look at how she relates to others and where she feels comfortable meeting new people. Through it all, mark how she's different from you.

4. **Let go of expectations -** Your child might love ballet for a whole week. Then, suddenly, no more tutus or ballet slippers. It's easy to start thinking, "She'll be a prima ballerina one day!" and completely forget that a kid's interests come and go like the weather. Practice staying present and focusing on what's happening today, not what might happen tomorrow.

5. **Let go of your fears -** Parents feel terrified most of the time. One mother came to me for an emergency session shaking with terror. "I think my daughter could be a lesbian!" she sobbed.

Together, we talked about her fear. What would it mean if her daughter was gay? How would it affect her life and her family? I encouraged her to try accepting her daughter the way she was, not push any shame or guilt onto her, and take her at face value. We talked about how building up trust between parents and children meant not judging one another and learning to love all of our differences.

6. **Be aware of underlying causes of behavior -** Pay attention to how your child acts when she's scared, stressed, or simply has an ADHD issue. Some days will go well and let you get comfortable, but don't think any problem has magically resolved. Treat each moment as its own thing, completely separate from the day before or even a few hours earlier. Raising kids is a roller coaster ride, so try to look for the peaks and valleys and focus on anticipating them and understanding what they mean for your child.

Learn to Relax and Help Your Kids Relax

For ADHD kids, quiet time is non-negotiable. You can guide your child through it and practice a few minutes each day to start, then build up to an hour or so. Don't feel pressured to fill every moment of the day with activities, but rather add solo time to your child's schedule.

Here are a few ideas to get you started:

- Listen to calming music - Try music without words, like classical tunes, or just music in a different language. That lets your child's mind relax.
- Create a quiet corner - Set aside a particular space for doing nothing. Add pictures of nature, an essential oil diffuser, comfy pillows, coloring books, and a source of slow, relaxing music.
- Combine story time and downtime - Choose stories with beautiful illustrations you can enjoy together, read the same story over and over, or choose something slow-paced to focus on relaxation.
- Try a mindful nature walk - Go out into a nearby park or preserve and take in all the space's shapes, colors, and sounds. Sit in one spot and use all five senses to experience the outdoors, then wander around and see if you hear, see, smell, or feel anything different.

Helping Kids Accept Themselves

Kids naturally compare themselves to others their age. They also worry a lot about how many friends they have, why they aren't more popular, and if their friends really like them or just like something about them.

A few different clients of mine cringe at the thought of how much better their peers are at putting together cool outfits, who had a better birthday party, or why someone chose a different friend over them. I try to use these opportunities to get young people to shift their language about themselves. Instead of digging into the negative, we flip the narrative and talk about what makes them great.

For example, one of my boys went out for the baseball team only to discover he lacked the skill to hit the ball. It was all he could think about.

"I have to leave the session early today and go practice batting with my friend," he told me. "I suck!"

I tried to get him to change that statement. I never disagreed with him or told him something untrue; his batting average was relatively low, and he needed to address it. But, I also wanted to hear him say what he did well.

"What about your position? Aren't you in the right field?" Yes, he confirmed; he played that position and occasionally shortstop.

"Well," I said, "that tells me you have a lot of strengths. It sounds like you're good at catching, fielding ground balls, and hopefully tagging out anyone who runs by you or tries to steal a base. That's incredible!"

We used that session to cover the problem of focusing on our weaknesses. Digging into what we can't do or describing ourselves as someone who "sucks" at something can build a dangerous, lasting internal narrative. And that changes how we see ourselves, which is the key to building a happy, healthy life.

As a parent, you can do a lot to help your ADHD kid see themselves as the amazing person they are with some simple practices at home. Let your child know she can give herself compliments and focus on her strengths. If another girl had a bigger, more well-attended birthday party, try to get your daughter to focus on what she loved most about her own party. Talk about how much fun she had, all the silly pictures she and her friends took together, and the memories they made.

Another great thing to practice is being loud and proud about what makes us unique. Ask your friends and family to video themselves and talk for about 15 seconds about something that sets them apart as a person. It could be, "I'm very short," or "I have a lot of freckles." Explain that it can be something they aren't 100 percent comfortable with yet, and the exercise should help them feel better about who they are. Then ask them to send you the videos.

Show the video to your kid, and then ask him to make his own. What's different about him? Is it only ADHD, or is it his curly hair? Could it be the color of his eyes? Ask him to try and pinpoint one thing he thinks makes him stand out from everyone else.

Exercises like that show kids that there's no such thing as fitting in or being normal. We all have things about ourselves that make us different. Letting your child focus on his unique traits can help him feel connected to others and help him see how great it is to be different.

Another great thing parents can do to facilitate self-acceptance is to avoid general statements about how your kid performed or competed in an activity. The next time you observe your child playing or watch a school play, pick two or three positive things to mention to your child.

Try saying things like, "I saw you choose to play with those nice girls over there by the swings and not that mean boy who got in trouble. You have great instincts about people!" If your child performs in a production or presents something, point out one moment like, "you said that funny joke about the witch, and everyone laughed. It was so funny!"

Avoiding general compliments like "great" or "good job" and focusing on specifics helps kids find what they're good at and celebrate those strengths. Don't hesitate to point out their natural talents.

The Benefits of Accepting Ourselves

It doesn't feel imperative to accept ourselves, but trust me, the benefits are endless. When we know ourselves better and accept the people we are, we're less likely to hide those actual traits. We've all met people who fake their way through life. These are people who have no idea where their strengths and weaknesses lie. Or, they choose to ignore that natural part of themselves and focus on pleasing others.

Kids who learn to love themselves are also learning to trust themselves. They make better decisions and don't hesitate to ask for what they need. They know that little voice in their head saying, "Don't be friends with those guys," or "This is your chance to get a cool summer job," is something they need to listen to, not ignore.

You may experience this yourself as you come to terms with who you are as a person and learn to celebrate yourself instead of working to change your current state. Imagine if we all just loved ourselves. Wouldn't that be incredible?

How ADHD Will Affect Your Child's Life

ADHD can change a lot of daily life. So, what are these new things we need to accept? Here's a quick look at some of the things you need to prepare for after your son or daughter gets diagnosed.

- **Compulsive eating -** In an effort to restore dopamine levels, many people with ADHD gorge on junk food, sugar, or carbs. This helps give them a rush of happiness that they might not feel otherwise.
- **Anxiety -** Thoughts and fears about the future can be like burrs in the ADHD brain. Once an

ADHD person starts to worry, it can be hard to stop.
- **Possible substance abuse -** Many medical professionals feel there may be a link between alcohol or drug abuse and ADHD. Because people with this disorder tend to be thrill-seekers and act impulsively, it may contribute to their desire to get high or drunk.
- **Chronic stress -** Managing ADHD is stressful! Over the years, many people with ADHD get physical symptoms like muscle pain, headaches, and bad stomachs due to their ongoing issues.
- **Screen addiction -** We all like to hang out online or binge a show, but this becomes a problem when we can't put our devices down. Some people with ADHD need help managing their screen time because the colors, graphics, and storylines get too fascinating for them and they can't walk away.
- **Emotional outbursts -** You'll likely see this one the most. ADHD makes managing anger or frustration extremely hard, and your child will need a lot of help from you to learn how to avoid screaming or lashing out when they feel big emotions.

Helping Kids Navigate the World

I listed the issues you're most likely to face above because anticipating those problems means you're more likely to navigate them with confidence when they occur. If you know your child is more stressed than the average kid, you can focus on de-stressing. Avoiding a binge eating session can be as simple as keeping junk food out of the house. But what about helping kids feel better about their lives as people with ADHD?

One thing I like to do is encourage problem-solving and discourage parents who want to rescue their kids. We all feel the need to jump up and stop a little one from falling or tell our kids how to handle a situation, but I want you to try letting your kid go it alone, at least once.

Problem-solving is a skill we need a lifetime to build up, and kids with learning disabilities are no different. The critical thing to do is show them that you're there as a sounding board, not to intervene. One mom who kept jumping in to solve her son's problems agreed she would take a step back after weeks of me insisting she was not teaching her son anything. He was only five and struggling socially, but I insisted she let him struggle and then encouraged him to talk about what happened with her.

"Practice reflection instead of deflection," I said one million times. Finally, after one million and one, she heard me.

"I saw another little boy push him down on the playground. No one got hurt, but he came crying and told me to give the other boy a spanking! Instead, we talked about how he felt and if it's better to stay away from someone who pushes people."

The two focused on how bad it felt to be around hurtful people and then used their vantage point on the bench to choose another potential playmate. The mom asked what might be the advantage of leaving mean kids behind and only playing with fun kids, which her son told her would be "much better."

She stayed on the bench and let him go and talk to a new group of kids. Soon they were all playing tag, and she did nothing to facilitate that game. They walked home together feeling like two champs.

If you want a confident kid, it's essential to let him try and problem solve. Encourage him to look back on the situation or predict what might happen if he tries a particular approach. What if he goes and pushes that boy who pushed him first? Would that be okay, or could it cause a big problem?

Another wonderful thing to focus on is any odd interest your child may have. Even if you don't entirely understand your daughter's obsession with Japanese baton twirlers, make room for it in your week. Watch a video together, let her tell you about her favorite performers, buy her a baton that looks like the one her favorite twirler uses. Seeing you respect her interests will make her respect herself and affirm that what she loves has value.

The thing to avoid is overreacting, yelling, or letting your frustration get the better of you when managing your child's ADHD. Remember, your kids look to you to see how you handle life's most challenging moments. If you resort to screaming, storming off, or reaching for a drink, eventually, they will, too.

Alternatives to Medication

Once your child gets diagnosed, you'll get a list of medications to be taken at specific times and for different issues. If you don't feel medication is the right move or if you want to combine medication with some good, healthy practices, here are some things to keep in mind.

- **Sleep, exercise, and a healthy diet** - A scheduled bedtime, regular exercise, and planned, healthy meals can significantly affect an ADHD child's life.
- **Try music therapy** - Music helps children flex their executive functions in their brains. Singing, playing a stringed instrument, or learning to appreciate a specific artist or genre can help stimulate new parts of the brain and practice sitting and listening.
- **Incorporate Omega-3s into your child's diet** - On top of healthy, balanced meals, you can focus on foods like walnuts, salmon, flax seeds, and leafy greens to help your child feel better. While

there's no official word on how this supplement can help ADHD, many medical professionals agree there does seem to be a connection between more attention and a diet high with these nutrient-rich foods.
- **Guided meditations -** Find some age-appropriate, short meditations and do a practice session with your kid once a day. It helps get anxiety and stress down, makes kids more aware of their actions, and helps them practice thinking before they act.

Chapter Summary

I hope this chapter gave you lots of new ideas. Here are some highlights:

- Remember that love and self-acceptance are at the heart of mental health for all kids.
- Work on your own self-judgment to help your child avoid judging herself.
- Let your kid express his interests, solve his problems, and reflect on his actions to build good cognitive skills.

4

REMOVE THE OBSTACLES

The first thing to do is mobilize as a family, a single unit made up of individuals. Try to give everyone involved a role to play, even if it's running around outside with your hyperactive child to help her blow off steam. Make sure everyone understands the mission at hand, to help someone who is atypical, and at the same time value what they have to say about it.

Why do all of this? Because a solid family base helps children feel confident and grow up to be successful individuals. It also helps them see their family members as a network full of helpers and people that can be supportive in the future. Establishing that give and take requires practice and patience, but I know you can do it.

Understanding Societal Expectations

Many ADHD kids' parents stress over how hard their child struggles to do primary socialization. They forget to say hello to new people. They blurt out random thoughts about someone's appearance or grab something that caught their attention.

One mother came to me feeling incredibly stressed about how her boss felt about her as a mother and teacher. "We went to my boss's house for dinner and Timmy, (not his real name) became obsessed with her jewelry. She leaned down to shake his hand, and he grabbed her brooch! The only reason it didn't rip through the fabric is that I managed to stop him, but it was awful!"

I encouraged Timmy's mom to try some role play at home and discuss why it's important to do things like meet and greet others politely. I suggested they cover things like what to do if someone's house is full of toys or significantly larger than our own, handle a tray of snacks meant for everyone, or behave in a playroom apart from the adults.

It never hurts to practice these things. When kids are impulsive, they benefit immensely from playing out scenarios. I recommend practicing the following: meeting and greeting someone new, how to wait to speak in a conversation (and how to politely interrupt if necessary), what to do with our face and body when we pay attention, thinking before acting, and playing in a group.

Timmy's mother took my advice, and together, she and her husband dressed up to play "grown-ups" with their son. Mom wore a suit, and Dad wore a big purple gown and a wig to make it fun. They let their son create a character and then played out different scenarios. Timmy's parents pointed out any successful interactions after visiting imaginary parties, hobnobbing at invisible art galleries, and pretending to be millionaires. If Timmy dropped the ball on paying attention or interrupted someone, they just asked him to try that conversation again. As soon as Timmy lost interest, they stopped playing and took a break.

To my client's surprise, Timmy loved the game. He asked to play Grown-Ups almost every day. With guidance from his parents and a low-pressure set-up, he understood social interactions much better and felt confident knowing what to do in most situations.

How to Deal with Peer Pressure

I know. This is the scary one. Parents with over-impulsive kids lose a lot of sleep over peer pressure. ADHD kids are always looking for the next exciting, dangerous thing, and you can't be looking over your child's shoulder all day. The truth is, other kids will have access to things you don't want in your son or daughter's life. Be it sugar, alcohol, drugs, or porn, kids will always find the things we don't want them to have.

I believe that rather than hide your child from the world, it's best to prepare them for it with open, honest discussion. The more you tell your kid the truth, the more he'll let you know about what's really happening at school or a friend's house. However, if you sugarcoat things about what it's like to drink, do drugs, or get hooked on internet porn, your kids will go find the truth without you. You don't want that. Trust me.

Peer pressure is something you'll need to deal with long before your son or daughter has a social group. Kids of all ages get pressured to do all kinds of things they don't want to but feel they should in order to have friends. One of my younger clients felt compelled to give away her cookies at lunch in exchange for a spot at a group's table, only to learn they had no interest in letting her sit with them.

Here are a few things you can do when your child comes to you about issues at school, with friends, or in other social situations:

1. Share some of your own experiences. Talk about times someone tried to shove a cigarette at you or made you feel like you had to lie to your parents. Make sure to include whether or not that person remained your friend after that intense experience and how it felt to stand up to someone.
2. Stay calm whenever your child talks about a classmate who wants them to do something they

don't like. Remember, your child came to you because she trusts you, not to watch you freak out. Take deep breaths, get as much information as possible, and assess the situation together.

3. Talk openly about friendships, how they should make us feel, and how they can backfire. Everyone will have a destructive or manipulative friend in their life. Make sure your child knows he isn't obligated to anyone; he can always walk away from a bad friend.
4. Also, discuss true independence whenever you can. Present independence as something to strive for and be proud of. Let them know independent people make decisions based on what lifts them up, not what others expect. Be sure to give examples, good or bad, from your own life.
5. Try some role-play, model, or saying no as a family. Practice a negative or a positive outcome - saying no could end a friendship, or it might blow over. Encourage your child to find friends who can handle a no or express no themselves because they know it's not smart to always agree with everyone.

I Don't Want My Child to Feel Alone!

Another major fear for many parents is that their child will be a loner. The status of an outsider can be positive for some people, but most kids ache to fit in. I have clients who spend hours staring at classmates' social media pictures in a desperate attempt to know what to wear, what food to eat, where to hang out.

A child's drive for social acceptance makes it especially heartbreaking when they discover they don't fit in, at least not with the people they already know. Many kids have to explore to find their tribe, which can be time-consuming, while others simply walk into a room and bang! Instant friends.

The teenage years are filled with social perils. Every outfit, decision to join a team or club, and hairstyle seem to signify something, and all teenagers want to send the right message. All teens spend their days painfully aware of how they look and interact with others and where they fall short, so try to approach yours with sympathy. They're all struggling.

Try not to encourage your teen to forget about everyone around him and just be himself. This could come across the wrong way. One young man told me, "My parents don't think I should have any friends!" simply because they'd try to convince him that being super popular isn't important. They were right, of course, but that idea feels alien to a teenage brain. At this point in life, the number one goal for humans is social connections, so the thought of putting them aside feels ludicrous.

Instead of shrugging off social drama, try to help your child understand it. He might have social barriers in place for any number of reasons.

Everything from autism, an extremely high IQ, or a deep love of TV chefs can set a kid apart. Other differences like being an ethnic minority, gender exploration, or questioning their sexuality can all add to the difficulty of fitting in.

Make sure all of these things are subjects you can discuss at home. If your child is the only one from Pakistan or the only trans student at school, be the sounding board. Let her know she can talk about it with you whenever they feel frustrated or alone.

Then, try to find some other kids in the same situation. Celebrate what makes her different and show her how much more it makes you love her and connects her to others in her community. Don't expect this to happen right away; it can take months, but don't give up. Some kids need more guidance than others to find friendship, so keep at it.

Limiting Beliefs

Kids can have crippling beliefs about themselves if we aren't careful. Thoughts that limit our kids can come from media, friends, or even an off-hand comment. They often don't come from parents. Adults do the same thing, but if we can catch these beliefs in our kids before they cement in a child's mind, we can give them a significant advantage.

To do this, you need to identify what your child thinks about herself and why. As kids don't often realize the ins and outs of a mental state, you have to be creative in your investigation.

The Huffington Post printed a long list of questions in 2018 that I love. It's too long to copy straight out, so I'll put my favorites here, and I'll link to the entire article in the Sources section of this book.

Here's my top ten:

1. What can you do now that you couldn't do before? (Run fast, shoot a basketball, draw a face)
2. What do all successful people have in common? (This question is meant to show your child there are things she'll need to investigate to understand better)
3. Which child from your class could be a future president? Why?
4. Can money always buy you happiness? Why/why not?
5. What would you look like if you woke up tomorrow morning twenty years older than you are today? (The answer to this will tell you a lot about how your child sees herself now)

6. Do you think it's possible to be automatically good at something? Automatically bad?
7. What does it mean to fail at something?
8. If a friend of yours failed to reach her goal, what would you tell her? Why?
9. If there was a zombie attack at your school, who would survive and why?
10. What would you change if you were President of the World for one day? Why?

Feel free to write your own questions. Just try not to be too direct, and don't be afraid to make them a little silly. One of my clients has a son with a passion for superheroes, so they talk a lot about how superpowers let us imagine ourselves succeeding in places we might otherwise fail. If we can be invisible, we're only seen when we want to be visible. If we can fly, we always have a way to leave a situation, etc.

How to Address and Overcome Limiting Beliefs

To catch a limiting belief in action, you need to know how to spot them. These can come out as filters we put on different situations like "this is too hard for me." Once we see something as nothing but challenging, we don't want to pursue it.

Another sign is negative self-talk. This happens when someone believes they're too small, too young, too old, too stiff, not creative enough, or any description of themselves to get out of trying something new. My ADHD kids often tell me something isn't working out at school because "I'm not smart like the other kids." That's heartbreaking to hear, but it also lets me know where to start with my younger clients.

The most powerful thing that keeps a limiting belief alive is a dangerous personal narrative. Some kids go through life convinced they're terrible people and don't deserve friends or love. As you can imagine, that belief opens the door to abusive friends and partners and needs to be corrected right away. Our personal narratives are often the things we're most embarrassed to talk about, so don't be surprised if your child doesn't want to tell you what he thinks of himself.

To leave these damaging thoughts behind, we need to find the moment that kicked them off. A lot of limiting beliefs stem from micro-traumas in our lives. If you hear your child express the idea that he's unintelligent, unworthy, or unlovable somehow, try to find out what formed that perspective. Did a teacher say something? Did he overhear parts of a conversation? Stay open to any source; most parents are pretty shocked when they learn why a child believes something with his whole heart despite only hearing or seeing it once.

Once you have the source, try to get as many details of that memory as you can. What day of the week was it? Where was your child? What did he wear that day? See how many details he can remember and then get into how things felt, who said what, and the more complicated things to discuss. Again, be patient. Then explain to your child how the stories he tells himself can sometimes hurt him, but it doesn't have to. Memories can also help us move forward.

Start by acknowledging and thanking the memory. You can write it all out on a piece of paper and say thank you to the written words, or he can do this quietly in his mind. This memory didn't mean to be negative. It wanted to keep him safe and happy. Then, release it. Rip up the paper. Burn it. Let him imagine it flying out of his mind, anything to let it go.

After it's gone, write it again with a new filter. Focus on the positive parts of the story. Say things like, "You wanted to cry because you're a kind, sensitive person, and I love that about you," or "You made new friends after that boy was mean to you; that's very smart." Try to put an uplifting spin on the tale to keep things in perspective.

Moving forward, keep the dialogue open on how comments about ourselves can help or hurt us. Does that thing you just said make you feel better or worse? Are you focusing on the frustrating part or trying to learn something new? Ask those questions a lot, and be ready to practice what you preach! Once your kids know how to spot limiting beliefs, they'll see yours in no time.

Everyone Has a Different Learning Style, and That's Okay

For reasons I still don't understand, we love to let small children explore and discover things at their own pace in preschool and kindergarten, but for some reason, we hesitate to let them continue as they get older. Instead, we force everyone into the same system at the same rate, no matter their learning style. It's incredibly frustrating, but it also pushes us to learn more about ourselves.

Discussing and Finding Our Unique Learning Styles

Learning styles can fall anywhere on a broad spectrum. Some people love to sit and read for hours, taking careful notes and highlighting favorite phrases, while others love to be in big noisy groups debating ideas. When I took Spanish classes, I recorded each lesson and then reviewed it by listening to the lecture on my walk home. Other students sang songs in Spanish or drew comics to help them learn new vocabulary.

Pay close attention to your child so that you can find her style. She can be a mix of visual, auditory, reading and writing, social, or kinesthetic (physical) learning, and it's up to you to help her pinpoint her strengths.

To start, notice what she chooses to do in her free time. If all she wants to do is run in circles in the front yard, try teaching her something while you go out on a walk. If it works, you know she responds well to kinesthetic learning. If you can set her in front of a video and walk away, then ask her about what she learned; she's visual. If she loves to write or read stories, that's a big part of her style, too.

Some kids have a tendency towards naturalism or the need to classify things the way a botanist might name the genus of different plants. Kids with a naturalist's brain like to identify things like different classifications of dinosaurs or the distinct sounds of cars, and they love to organize. You'll know if you get a big reaction after putting a toy in the wrong color box that you have a naturalist.

If you have a hard time nailing down your child's style, ask for some outside help. Sometimes we need another perspective to help us better look at a problem. One family came to me begging for help with a boy who "loved chaos" and seemed incapable of functioning unless two TVs and a song were all on at once and only with the family present.

I explained to them that he was an auditory learner, someone whose brain was geared towards learning with sound, and they should find a way to get him some noise. They bought him a nice pair of headphones and helped him remember to take one off if he needed to hear the people around him. They also asked his teacher if they could please make an audio recording of her class so he could review it at home. He loved the recordings so much he made them at recess and eventually started doing a little radio play with some of his friends.

If you think you might have the wrong learning style for your child, try some experiments at home. Ask your kid if she can draw something for a lesson or story, if she can act it out, or try reading a story that ties in with what she's learning. You'll know if you've hit on the right style if she wants to do it again after her homework is done.

Technology and Distraction

I understand that technology is a massive part of life and can be incredibly helpful. But I also met many parents who seem to think it's impossible to get their child to enjoy time outside or read a book. The more I work with kids, the more I find this is simply not true. Remember, technology is a resource, not a way of life, so it's crucial for parents to relay that message to their kids.

We can limit how many things get thrown at us as consumers. I recommend downloading ad blockers and anti-ghost apps to keep big data companies from advertising to you and your kids at all times. I use these on my computer and can watch a YouTube video with no ads. When kids see an uninterrupted video, it helps them focus on the message or the lesson and doesn't break up their concentration.

Then, think about how you use technology. Do you like to sit and scroll on your phone for a long time, play mindless games, or flip through random Instagram posts? If so, expect your children to do the same. But, if you use your phone to keep track of your schedule, read books and articles, or video yourself out with your family, your kids will start to mimic those behaviors.

One great example of how use can shift with smartphones is BookTok. BookTok started on TikTok, the super-short video app that helps kids quickly create and share tons of content. Some reading fans got on the app to review books and share their love of super-niche fiction, and soon, book sales were through the roof! Here were a bunch of Gen Z kids, none of whom thought they could be avid readers, running to bookstores to grab novels from their favorite influencers!

What You Can Do as a Parent to Help Limit Technology Time

To start, I encourage you not to let a child have a smartphone or excessive screen time before 13. Brain development in a young child's early years is crucial. Allowing your child to play video games, spend time with a touch screen, or use your phone can create a screen addiction. Opt for paperback books, crafts, wooden toys, or art supplies to help your child develop critical thinking skills.

I make exceptions for video calls with family. If your child sees the laptop as a glorified phone, it's not a toy. Also, you can develop a system for making calls to

Grandma and talk about how great it is that technology lets us see people who are far away. Sometimes parents need a break and reach for a trusted, kid-friendly movie or educational video for the kids.

Keeping kids offline also helps keep them away from inappropriate material that might be overly sexual or violent. The threat of online predators is genuine, so having your child stay offline can also protect them from online grooming (a long, slow process that almost ends in sexual abuse in person or over the internet).

But what about kids over 13? Talk about this with your partner and decide what you want to have as your family phone policy. Should phones only be for times when you're separated as a family, only be used for emergencies? Are smartphones even necessary? You can start with a flip phone that only makes and receives calls to help your child develop good habits and show that they're responsible.

Another option is to take tech breaks. Maybe an hour of homework gets rewarded with a thirty-minute tech break. Many teachers do this in class to stem students' anxiety about missing essential updates or messages.

You can also find ways to use your child's favorite sites and apps to your advantage. If she loves YouTube, ask her to show you some of the content she likes and tell you why she likes it so much. You can challenge her to make videos for class, create a written response to a video, and start a critical thinking dialogue about why that particular creator appeals to her.

The same can happen with video games. Check out games as a family and talk about why it's not a good idea to use any chat or social add-ons to the game. Instead, focus on the plot of the game and work through it. If there are cut scenes or moments when the game becomes a video, tell your child he has to watch them and take in the whole story. Then set time limits with games - one hour of gaming means another hour outside doing some exercise - and explain why.

All of this is to say that technology doesn't have to be your enemy. It can be the tool that helps you talk to your kids about how hard you work to protect them, the dangers of life online, their brain development, the importance of not sitting for extended periods, you name it. Create limits, be consistent and model the behavior you want to see with technology and you'll be well ahead of the curve.

Life is Full of Obstacles, but the Obstacle is the Way

If you studied stoicism or any Eastern philosophy, you likely already know the previous phrase. Essentially, it means we have to be careful how we talk about our problems. If we find out something isn't going to happen, we have two choices. We can get upset and feel sorry for ourselves and hate our lives. Or we can shift our perception. We can say, "This is my situation. I need to learn something from this or find a way to enjoy it."

The stoics I know love the story of Thomas Edison and his factory. Edison had a vast, successful factory that suddenly caught fire, and the whole thing burned to the ground. He got out (and I believe his workers did as well), and his son ran to meet Edison while the man stared at the disaster. Edison didn't cry or fall to the ground in despair. Instead, he told his son, "Go get your mother and her friends. They've never seen a fire like this."

The idea that our workplace burning can be a reason to gather and stare at the spectacle is stoicism in practice. Yes, you can be upset that your factory is burning down; that's a normal reaction. But it's important to remember that tears don't put out a fire. Instead, we have to remove ourselves from danger, take a moment, and see what we can do to solve the problem. Edison used his burned-down factory as a way to change how he worked. What can you and your child do with ADHD? Teach your child that obstacles are simply opportunities in disguise and watch their power grow.

Examples of Positive Belief Structures

I want to tell you about three different kids I know through my practice. I love these stories because all of them show how with ADHD, the obstacle is the way.

Ben - I met little Ben when he was four. His doctor diagnosed him the same week his parents brought him to meet me, and I liked Ben immediately. He took one look at the miniature airplanes in my office and didn't want to talk about anything else. He told me how planes go high, how people ride inside them, how some planes fight in the sky.

His parents felt incredibly nervous about this. He tried to fly around his daycare like he had wings! He didn't want to look at anything that wasn't a plane! What could they do?

"Try to build on this interest," I told his parents. "Comment on how focused he is and how much you admire that. Change the conversation, so it's about his ability to pay attention to one thing for a long time rather than punishing him for loving something."

Once he and his parents started to enjoy his obsession with planes, he spoke with them more. His mom even got him to eat healthier foods by serving them on special trays that made everything look like airplane food.

Then, when it was time to focus on something else, his parents reminded him that he knew how to focus. It was up to him to put that brainpower into a new subject. It took practice, exercise, and lots of mindfulness, but he got there eventually.

Samantha - Samantha came to me when she was in fifth grade. Her teachers worried she was distracting other students. Sam liked to kick chairs and interrupt when the teacher spoke, sometimes even breaking out into songs during a lesson.

"She's about to get expelled," her dad confided in me. I wondered if maybe her school was the wrong place for her. Would he consider an art school, something where she could express herself more freely?

I shortlisted some schools with good drama programs, and Sam and her dad took a few tours. Sam fell hard for a school that used theater to teach a myriad of subjects and had teachers who, while they loved theater, also made sure their classes stayed orderly and in control. She enrolled and studied there for years. Her ADHD helped her improvise tons of stories that she wrote down as she got older. Now she's going to college to learn about scriptwriting.

Gary - Gary came to me as a frustrated teenager. He had no friends. No one would even look at him on campus, and he never had a girlfriend. The only place he found community was online.

I talked to him about what appealed to him about talking to his online friends. He explained he loved reading fan fiction articles and watching videos about doing new things. I watched him as he broke down how to take 360-degree photos and then turn them into a digital tour. He lit up! This was something very special to him.

Gary's case was unique because he was about to graduate and didn't struggle too much in school. His problem came from disconnection and boredom. I went online with him and challenged him to find digital groups that met for group video calls or possibly in-person once in a while.

"I want you to practice your social skills," I explained to him. "I'll help you, but the best way to practice interacting with others is to just go for it."

He was reluctant, so I asked his parents to help him practice. Together we encouraged him to find groups based on interest, like photography. He found a small group of people who created Virtual Reality walks through different cities and contributed a walk through his grandmother's hometown. The project opened some doors for him socially, and he started meeting up with groups that went out to photograph forgotten places, ghost towns, and abandoned buildings.

Before he knew it, Gary had a social group. Sure, it wasn't what he pictured at first, but it got him there. He eventually decided not to go to college but to focus on his trade and help realtors with virtual tours of houses. He does quite well.

Chapter Summary

I loved writing this chapter. My view on ADHD is quite positive, and I hope this section made you feel the same way!

- Remember that it's better to anticipate problems

and take a proactive stance to help you and your child succeed.
- Fight the trend of blaming technology and instead shift your relationship with electronics and the internet.
- Finally, the obstacle is the way.

5

DEVELOPING NEW BELIEF SYSTEMS AND HEALTHY ALTERNATIVES

A young boy I saw for a long time sat down in my office and told me not to bother working with him. "No one likes me," he said, "I'm sure you won't either," I asked him why he thought no one liked him. Did people say "I don't like you" to him regularly?

"One boy told me," he explained. "At school, I tried to play with some kids, but he stopped me. He said no one wanted to be my friend."

We had a long talk about why someone might say that. We talked about fear, jealousy, and anger.

"I think that boy noticed you're not like him and got nervous. He might have thought his friends would like you better than him."

That made him do a double-take. "But, no one plays with me."

"I bet there are a lot of kids who would love to play with you," I told him. "I think you're looking in the wrong places."

It's not easy to turn a child's self-esteem around, but it can be done. With my help, he found a group of friends who loved reading as much as he did and enjoyed playing sports. Once he bonded with other people, he saw how important it was to care about himself as much as he cared about others and how moping around doesn't change anything.

Help Your Child Develop New Belief Systems About Themselves

Self-esteem starts incredibly early. Early trauma in childhood, formative events at school, on the playground, and at home all feed our self-esteem meter. We're so attentive and impressionable at a young age. Many adults have crystal clear memories of rejection, humiliation, and cruelty that continue to inform their decisions. Even when in the womb, events that happen to our mothers can affect us and change how we see ourselves.

Your ADHD kid may face some judgment. You might even have to step in once in a while. All of that is okay as long as you maintain a good baseline of emotion and reaction. The critical thing is to not make anyone feel unloved or like a burden to the family in any way. Kids pick up on frustrations very fast. I often tell my adult clients that you simply can't lie to children. They see through the falsehood almost immediately.

Imagine your child gets distracted at dinner and spills gravy all over the table. Then he panics, walks away, or starts pacing the room in a panic. Yes, it's annoying that you'll have to clean all that up, but it's not the end of the world. The real problem is how your son feels about spilling and the fact that he's panicking.

Resist the urge to say something like, "Calm down!" or "You're overreacting!" These can feel dismissive and hurtful and do nothing to change the moment's energy. Instead, try:

"We all spill sometimes. It's okay. I'm going to clean this up and make you a new plate of food. You can come and join us at the table again whenever you're ready."

Your son might not come back to the table right away. Give him some space and make it clear you aren't angry. Keep a calm tone, talk to your family about something else, which gives him a moment of space. When he's ready, he'll sit down again. When you demonstrate calm and love in this way, you help a child see that he's loved, that he doesn't have to be perfect all the time, and that you accept him.

I talked about staying calm, observing, and asking questions earlier in the book, and I want to stress that doing those things have a long-term effect on how your kid feels about himself. It is vital to understand that he's not the center of everyone's problems, that everyone makes mistakes, and we can all continue to love each other through the bad stuff. And, it's essential to understand how your child feels about himself and replace any belittling beliefs with positive theories that lift him and carry him through life.

What Do Healthy Beliefs Look Like?

Healthy beliefs come from a lifetime of understanding ourselves, why we feel the way we do, and how those beliefs affect our actions. Our core beliefs are not things we say out loud necessarily. Instead, they tend to be things we express with a supportive belief that we tell ourselves.

For example:

My core belief is "I am unlovable." The supportive belief that I say to myself is, "Nobody loves me." You'll notice the belief starts with something about ourselves, or an I statement, then transfers to someone we see all around us. It's a great example of how we change our lives by maintaining a particular narrative about the world.

So, what do healthy beliefs make us say to ourselves? A core belief like "I am loved" or "I am accepted" can lead to supportive beliefs like:

- I can manage conflict respectfully.

- It's essential for me to express my needs - mine are as important as anyone else's.
- I feel good about standing up for what I believe.
- Expressing anger can sometimes be a step towards solving a problem.
- I can rely on my judgment and solve problems independently or with help.

How to Build a Healthy Relationship with Oneself

It can sound silly, but I often encourage my clients to think about their thoughts. This is a form of meta-communication or a way to deepen your self-knowledge. Note your thinking patterns, particularly about yourself. How you see and feel about yourself can be unbelievably transformational.

To demonstrate, let me tell you about Clara. Clara was a mom of two boys, both diagnosed with ADHD. She initially fought the diagnosis, got angry with anyone who tried to talk to her about her boys' behavior at school or potential long-term problems. It wasn't until a good friend of hers told Clara that she had ADHD and never got the proper support as a kid. Her friend implored Clara to help her sons and understand why she felt so offended by the idea of her children having a learning disability.

I started to meet with Clara weekly. Sometimes she came in alone, other days, she visited with her boys, or she just called me from time to time. It took her a long time to open up, but when she finally did, we pinpointed the heart of the issue. She always felt her mother's disappointment with her as a student. Clara never went to college, choosing a trade instead, as she wasn't much of an academic. It was clear to her that her mother felt she'd made a mistake.

"Mom just felt sure I could be valedictorian or the debate team champ or something like that, but I just wanted to work with my hands," she explained. We talked about how she had a certain kind of brain (she's a visual thinker) and not the one her mother hoped she'd have.

"You know," I told her, "you're in a position to accept these boys in a way you never got accepted yourself. That's very special."

How can you accept yourself and, eventually, your kids? It starts with a daily practice. Something as basic as complimenting your reflection is a great start. Some of my clients like to gaze deep into the mirror, stare into their own eyes and declare their love and acceptance of themselves.

Others insist it's a matter of not taking life so seriously. One of my clients told me, "My little two-year-old wreaks havoc and then laughed like a maniac. It used to drive me insane, but then I just started laughing with her. She taught me not to be so worried about a mess. Life's too short!"

Empowering Your Child to Take Charge of Their Education

I often ask parents, "What's your general attitude about school?" I find that, unlike me, most of my clients detested school. They see it as a place where kids are forced to do things they hate, get constantly judged and evaluated, and have to suffer through a massive list of chores to earn a few hours to do what they like.

Unfortunately, those same parents communicate that feeling of "I hate school" to their kids, often without even realizing they're doing it. I bet you know a few kids (possibly your own) who love to learn and see a school for what it is - a resource to help them find out more about the world. These are the kids who push themselves, who love to read, and who understand teachers are helpers, not enemies. If you want to get your kid to that point, there are a few things you can do.

First, involve your kids in your decision-making process. Tell them more about what you do at your job and ask for their advice. How would they handle a difficult boss? What about an angry client? Do they agree you should ask for that raise?

Another great tactic is to involve them in household functions. I tell all my clients to ask their kids to take over grocery shopping on some level. Older kids can help create the budget for your next visit to the store. Younger kids can practice writing by helping you make a list of what to buy. Investigate prices and quality together - do your kids agree with your shopping choices, or can they convince you to try something new or switch brands?

I also encourage you to learn something as a family. This can get tricky, so try to keep the topic light. I love hearing about families who take a string art class together or learn to make pasta as a group.

The important thing here is to model a love of learning for your kids. If we present school as fun, valuable and can show how learning extends beyond the classroom, we give them a considerable advantage. When they hear negative messages about school and learning from you, your children are more likely to consider school a waste of time. That only compounds the issues ADHD kids already experience.

How to Encourage Your Child to Communicate Their Wants and Needs with You

Effective communication seems to elude families at all times. I rarely meet a client who tells me, "Oh, my daughter tells me everything!"

Communication creates struggles between adults and children because kids think differently than adults. As parents, we often forget that and expect our kids to have our experienced, adult logic, not their own, unique view of the world still in development. That's not to say you can't create a good back and forth with your child. Kids at all stages of life, even babies, learn to communicate with their parents.

Here are some things you can practice with children between one and three years old to start a good dialogue between the two of you:

- When your baby nuzzles you, respond verbally. Say, "Oh, you must be hungry!" This teaches babies they can trust adults to respond to their non-verbal cues.
- When your baby stops eating his food and focuses on playing with it, comment, "Hey, looks like you're done eating. Let's go play with the blocks." This helps build your baby's confidence in his communication skills.
- A two-year-old might point and make a noise like "Ba! Ba!" over and over. Get down as close as you can to her eye level and explain, "I don't know what you mean, honey. Can you say it again?" When you realize she's pointing at the slide or another baby, say so. "Oh, you mean the baby! Yes, the baby is adorable." That teaches children that communication sometimes requires extra effort.
- A preschool-age child might want to process his day on the ride home, talking about snacks or

something funny that happened. Listen closely and ask follow-up questions as he describes everything. Show your child that you value his comments and appreciate when he talks to you.

How to Have Effective Conversations with Your Child

I know most of my readers have kids older than preschool, so I want to show how you can do the older, more advanced version of these things with middle or high-school-aged kids.

One of the best things you can do is read together. This gives you something in common and helps build on that love of learning we discussed in the previous section. Make sure your child picks out the books most interesting to her.

Another great practice is to factor in age when you make a request. For instance, teenagers hate hearing the exact instructions over and over again, but parents often feel they aren't heard if they only say something once. I encourage parents to state what they want and what will happen if their instructions aren't followed.

Try, "I need you ready to be out the door by 8:45 if you want a ride. If you aren't ready by that time, you have to walk to school." Then, don't say anything. Wait and see what happens. If your kid makes it to the door, completely ready and on time, take her to school. If not, don't repeat yourself. Walk out and let her get herself to school. By not repeating yourself, you show her that you mean what you say, you expect her to listen, and that you'll reward responsible actions. It also shows her you trust her to get to school independently after you leave.

Above all else, be a good role model. Put your phone away when people, especially family, speak to you. Make eye contact and turn your body to the person speaking. Ask follow-up questions and take what they say seriously. Let your kids see and hear what good communication looks and sounds like. Make sure they know that you gain a lot from a sincere conversation and appreciate it.

Teaching Them How to Positively and Effectively Express Themselves

It's great to show our kids that we can listen, but how do we get them to talk to us? I want to encourage you to make a goal of getting your child to open up about how she feels, verbally or otherwise, to better connect with her. You can do that through questions, good modeling, and offering alternatives to talking. Questions help parents learn more about their child's experience in the world. It can also help build empathy.

Use questions to reflect your child's emotions. Ask, "I think you're excited about your birthday - is that right?" When she confirms that yes, she's excited, say something like, "I can tell by the way you're jumping out of bed in the morning and checking the calendar!" That shows her she's got your attention and that you don't need her to spell it out for you - you can see the emotion.

Questions can help build empathy, too. When someone at school gets sick, hurt, or has a bad experience, ask your child to imagine how that kid feels.

"Richie hit his head on the playground. How do you think he feels?" Questions like this challenge your child to put themselves in someone else's frame of mind, something many kids struggle to do before reaching adulthood. Make sure you add your predictions to the situation and mention how much it means to people when we take the time to empathize.

Modeling can be as simple as telling your child a story. Tell him about yourself when you suspect your child wants to share something but might not have the vocabulary or confidence. That's not to say you should do all the talking - you have to feel this one out.

Many kids need to hear our own stories before they feel confident enough to jump into the conversation. After you talk about your own experience with a teacher, for example, he might say, "Yeah, that's what happened to me," or "Well, my teacher is different…." Then, hear him out.

Some kids just aren't talkers, and that's okay. Your child might be more of an introvert or just someone who thinks visually. Rather than fight her nature, try to meet her on her level. This back and forth of stories is a great way to keep the dialogue open and help your child see that he can trust you with the tough stuff.

Help your child find a visual medium, like painting or sculpture, to help her express how she feels. Or, give her something physical to do as a means of letting out her frustration, like smashing up old junk (safely), playing a contact sport, or going for long runs. If you think she might respond better to having a script, put her in a drama class or the local community theater. The opportunity to be someone else could be a considerable confidence boost.

Many kids feel heavily observed and shrink away from the world, even if friends and family are the only people paying attention. Explain that shyness is a normal human feeling and that they don't have to be social butterflies, but they need to be able to say what they're thinking or what they want. Helping your kids better understand themselves and their emotions takes a lot of practice, particularly when their heads are full of noise and energy. But, we have solutions for that as well.

Practices to Help Calm an Overactive Mind

A non-stop, fast-paced train of thought in the evening can spell disaster for a good night's sleep. Test anxiety can keep students from passing an exam, even when they know the material. The key is often relaxation, yet I don't often meet parents who teach their kids how to relax, even in the evening.

I know a lot of parents (including me) who rely on movies and TV shows in the evening to get their kids still and ready for bed. Many of those same parents use stories or a reading hour to help everyone calm down, and I've personally found this to be highly effective. Even e-readers can calm us down as their screens are designed to look like paper.

But what can we do beyond reading or staring at a movie? Don't worry - you have a lot of options. Start with breathing exercises. One option is to hold your left nostril closed and breathe through the right for two minutes. Take long, mindful breaths and feel how the one-side-only breath changes your state of mind. If you want your kids to do this, be ready to do it with them. Create a calming environment and play slow-paced music or light scented candles to create a unique space.

Younger children can practice taking in a great big breath, holding it for a few seconds, then blowing bubbles or blowing a piece of paper across the table. The trick here is to keep it calm, so make sure to explain why you're doing this activity and the goal - to help us calm down and relax. Some kids manage to get to sleep but can't stay in bed. Offer a few I-can't-sleep activities and encourage your child to quietly get out of bed and go into another space when this happens.

Set up a chair or small space and explain that everyone else is sleeping, so she needs to do any activity independently. Give her an audiobook track and some headphones so she can listen, a book to read, or a diagram of a breathing exercise she can follow. Discourage eating, drinking, wandering around the house, or anything that might keep her from going back to sleep.

Tips and Tricks for Dealing with ADHD in Today's World

Managing sleep is one of the many things ADHD kids need to learn how to do as they grow up. They also have to develop an awareness of time, how long they take to do essential tasks, and what distracts them.

There are tons of ways to manage ADHD, and I recommend you and your family try lots of different things to find what works best for your child. Here are some great tricks and tips to get you started.

School and Teacher/Parent Relationships

- Do your best to volunteer for school events and field trips, chaperone dances, or organize fundraisers. Schools are more likely to hear out parents who prioritize their school.
- Use teachers' first names (with permission). It

shifts the dynamic between you and the leader of the classroom.
- Show up to meetings on time and bring snacks. Many don't have time in between sessions to grab a meal. Teachers love it when parents respect their time and make them feel appreciated.
- Find a way to share positive feedback and observations with the teacher and encourage them to share with you. Some of my clients use an online document, and others have a daily card where the teacher can jot down notes, circle an emoji to show frustration or happiness, and make recommendations. Whatever you choose, make sure it doesn't take up more than five minutes of a teacher's day.
- Look for a good tutor or a school homework club (your child's teacher can even help you create one). This will take you out of the homework battle, often a source of many at-home arguments.
- Designate a neutral space for homework like the local library or a room at school where your child won't be distracted by TV, siblings, or toys.
- Block out the same time every day for homework, so it's never a surprise.
- Try to find something to do while your child works on her assignment. Read a book, organize a shelf, or work on your project from your boss, but don't check in every few minutes. Stay close

by without hovering. Give her space to do the work and then go over it when she's finished.

After school winds down and you can catch your breath, it's essential to get in some physical exercise (most of my ADHD clients find running, even a slow run, feels great), and then sleep. Again, schedule everything and set a time for how long a run or a play session can last.

Bedtime has to stay consistent, even as your child gets older. Many of my clients have great ideas for getting an ADHD kid ready for bed. Here are some of my favorites:

Going to Sleep

- Put your child to sleep in stages. Start with a bath, followed by a story. Then put on a CD or special playlist to help signal to your child that it's time for him to close his eyes.
- If you live in a high-traffic area, arrange your child's room, so the least amount of light possible comes in through the doorway or window. Use a fan or a white noise machine to drown out the sound of cars or people outside.
- Do a breathing exercise like 4-7-8. Breathe in for four seconds, hold it for seven, then exhale for eight. Repeat that until he's nice and calm.
- If your family is religious, try a bedtime prayer. Children like to hear about someone protecting

- them while they sleep, and the act of praying can add a dynamic element to the evening ritual. If you aren't religious, ask your child to say what he's grateful for out loud.
- Your child might respond well to a small dose of melatonin. Look for kid-friendly gummies that have a 5 mg dose of melatonin (the chemical our brains produce when we're tired), and have your child take it about 45 minutes before bedtime.

All of this is nice, but what about day-to-day issues and your response to the bad times? How do you discipline someone who already struggles to pay attention? Luckily, plenty of parents find ways to discipline their ADHD kids. I'm listing some of my favorites to help your discipline be clear, constructive, and calming for everyone involved.

Discipline

- Plan out problems and your response ahead of time. You can write yourself a script if you like. What will you say if your child gets in a fight or skips school?
- Try to approach each problem with a cop mentality. Did you notice the time? Let's check your schedule. Focus on the why and consider that she may not be aware of her actions or that she might not be aware she's lost a lot of time.

- Look for apps designed for kids with ADHD (at the time I wrote this, my favorite was Brili). A lot of these apps help them realize how long they take to do something with countdowns, changes in color, or activity tracking. It also lets you do what you need to do and helps your child become more independent.
- Take a timeout for yourself. If you feel yourself getting emotional or just angry, stand up and say, "I'm going to take five minutes to calm down," then walk out of the room. Start a timer and write down what you're feeling or meditate. Then, go back and discuss the problem. This sets an excellent example for ADHD kids - they learn that they can remove themselves from the situation.
- Keep words to a minimum. Rather than give long, drawn-out speeches about why we need to organize our things, try, "I want to help you organize your closet. Then, I want you to practice keeping it nice." Anything more complicated will cause your child's attention to wander.
- Use a calm voice and start with the emphasis on loving your child. Yelling breeds yelling, so avoid it whenever you can. Take a deep breath, remind yourself that your child needs your understanding.

How Do You Deal?

On top of helping your child, you also need to help yourself. It's essential that you care for your health, maintain a level of energy, and schedule time for your own peace of mind. This can be as little as five minutes a day, so make it count!

There are a few things you can do to maintain your sanity. First, you need a highly ordered household. I know a lot of parents who hate the idea of scheduling every hour of the day, but keep in mind that ADHD kids don't do well in changing environments. They need precise schedules, predictability, and support. This helps keep impulsive tendencies down.

Try a family calendar that shows where everyone is at different times of the day. Use color-coding, magnets, a whiteboard for notes, anything to help your child plan out a day and a week. Keep your house as clean as possible, plan out meals, budget your money. Make sure your family gets involved in this process to give you as much support as they can.

The next thing you need to keep in mind is to choose your battles. Before you tackle a situation, ask yourself, "Is this worth my time and energy?" If the answer is yes, take a deep breath and speak calmly and in short, clear sentences. Is the answer no? Take a moment to change the room's energy with a distraction or suggested activity. Then move on.

Use to-do lists, positive reinforcement, and low-distraction environments to help you and your child. ADHD kids love knowing what to expect and feeling they accomplished their goals for the day. Remember that ADHD kids get distracted by things other kids might ignore. Pay attention to any stimulating factors you can eliminate to make homework or a quiet time more effective. When your child does what he needs to, make sure you talk about how proud you are, offer up a high-five, or get his favorite pizza.

My favorite thing parents do is give their kids some unstructured time. Ironically, it has to be scheduled (free time, 5:30), then no activity in that section. Let your child know why that time is unstructured, where he can go, and when free time ends. Try a free window right before dinner to help him get some energy out, which in turn helps him sit still for an extended period.

Diet is a Crucial Factor

The way your child eats can help calm down her ADHD. Many parents find that dietary changes can change how a kid with ADHD interacts with others, her impulsivity, or her ability to relax.

Experiment with elimination diets. For example, choose one food, dairy, and take it out of your family's diet. Remember, tons of replacements are available no matter what you take out. You can make dairy-free cheese at home or find non-dairy milk in most stores. It will take more planning, but some extra effort will lead to massive returns.

Then, keep dairy out of your cooking, and don't go out for any cheesy or creamy foods for about two weeks. Watch your kids closely and see if your ADHD child shows any changes. If she does, you know that too much dairy will wind her up. No change? Add dairy back in and try eliminating something else like packaged, highly-preserved food or white sugar.

Many parents go with a whole diet or a diet high in fruits, vegetables, and whole grains with minimal animal protein. This is an excellent option for families who have access to good markets or a farmer's market once a week. Focus on in-season, locally grown foods if they're available to you. If that's not an option, do your best to focus on whole, unpackaged ingredients and keep your meals colorful. You know you've made a misstep if everything on the table is white and brown.

For parents who struggle to get good groceries or find they can't access a good selection of groceries, I recommend doing some gardening. Try to find plants that are easy to grow in your area and the easiest way to start them. You can buy seeds online or in stores with a gardening section. A little dirt in an eggshell is all you need to produce a seedling! Gardening takes time and patience, but there's an added benefit - it's an excellent activity for ADHD kids.

The time spent outside in the dirt, caring for plants, pulling weeds, and watching plants grow counteracts the impulsive part of the brain. It also gives you something you can do together, and the rewards develop right there, in front of you!

Redesigning Their Diet

Once you figure out what changes you want to make in your family's diet, you can start to monitor some aspects of your food.

First up is amino acids. Amino acids are often called the building blocks of protein. There are tons of different kinds, so I'll let you hunt down the specifics of this essential element. The vital thing to know is that you can get them in any lean animal meat or plant proteins, including tofu and gelatin. To up your amino acids, try adding pumpkin seeds, almonds, lamb, tofu, quinoa, or homemade gelatins to your family meals.

Kids with ADHD struggle to keep their levels of zinc, magnesium, calcium, and phosphorus up. You can help them balance out with supplements (or a multivitamin), or you can look for some foods high in each. Zinc is found in milk, oysters, red meat, chickpeas, assorted nuts, and baked beans. Many boxed cereal will have added zinc, but beware of the high amounts of sugar. Try leafy greens, nuts, seeds, dry beans, whole grains, wheat germ, wheat, and oat bran for added magnesium. You can get calcium from dairy, but you can also find it in: seeds (chia, poppy, and sesame), sardines, salmon, beans, lentils, and almonds. Leafy greens also give us lots of calcium, but be careful not to rely solely on spinach and lettuce. Experiment with kale, Asian greens, mustard greens, and okra.

All of the foods listed above also contain phosphorus. Don't be fooled! You might find packaged or processed foods that claim to have lots of phosphorus, but this is a synthetic version of the real thing.

I highly encourage families to sit and plan meals together. We're so lucky to have resources all over the web to help us cook and eat better. Take advantage of online cooking videos, food experts, and bloggers to help get everyone excited about changes in the family diet. Look for better, healthier versions of old favorites like fried chicken or homemade pizza. Be open to feedback, too. If you're going to change how everyone eats, you'll have to hear about it.

Help Them to Set Goals and Accomplish Them

Apart from nutrition goals, your child needs your help setting and working towards his unique goals. For ADHD kids, those goals can be as simple as delaying gratification, not getting frustrated, or not fighting with their siblings. He may want to do something new, like learn a song on the piano or figure out how to draw his favorite character.

Take those goals seriously. Your child wants to feel supported and will look to you and your partner before he looks to anyone else. Discuss his goals together and look for ways to work towards them. If you feel your child is too young to pursue those dreams, consider how one-year-old babies learn to walk. They take one shaky step and realize, "Oh! I can walk! I don't have to crawl anymore. I want to try that again." He goes on to practice every day until finally, he walks.

If a growing baby can devote himself to the goal of walking, your six or seven-year-old can work towards what she wants. It's important to show her that setting a goal, making a plan, and working towards it is a worthwhile practice. It also teaches her perseverance so she'll be less likely to give up when life or work gets tough.

Start with identifying your child's role. Help her see how she interacts with different people - she's a daughter, a sister, a niece, a grandchild, a neighbor, etc. Then, start a conversation about how she can improve those relationships. Could she be a more patient sister? What about a more attentive granddaughter or a more helpful neighbor?

Once she has those big, conceptual goals, talk to her about steps to achieve them. A patient sister is someone who plays what her younger sibling likes, someone who doesn't fight for toys, who uses a calm voice. Write down three or four small, achievable goals for becoming a better sister, and then give each a timeline (I like a week).

Then come up with a visual signal that her goal was achieved. Many families like to give a colorful sticker if their child makes some progress for the day. The card or page with the days of the week and the stars marking success stays up on the wall in an appropriate place. Some kids feel odd about sharing their goals, while others like to keep them where the whole family can see their progress.

If your child earns five or more stickers, that's a success and requires a celebration. You might cheat on your healthy diet with a round of ice cream or go to a place your child likes. Make sure she's clear why she got a reward - she worked hard and earned it. Then let her know how proud you are and want to help her achieve more goals.

Keep a close eye on possibilities for your child. If she says something like, "I wish I could dance," talk to her about how people learn to dance. Discuss the importance of starting slow, building the basics, and then slowly challenging themselves as they develop their skills.

Offer to help her make a plan and then follow through. When you pursue these flights of fancy, you get a chance to help your child foster a can-do attitude and develop a good sense of self. Even if she doesn't become a prima ballerina, she's someone who went after a goal and did her best. That's worthy of admiration.

Chapter Summary

- Remember, it's important to investigate what your child believes about himself and why.
- Foster an environment of transparent, open communication and mutual respect so your children can learn to manage their emotions.
- Tackle good practices like eating healthy food and working towards goals every day.

6

YOUR CHILD IS A SPONGE

You already know what good copycats kids can be. Children start to imitate their parents in their first year of life. Toddlers love to pull credit cards out of wallets and "shave" in front of the mirror, just like Mom and Dad.

That mimicry doesn't stop at two years old. We need to remember that the environment we create at home, the habits we build, the words we say - all of these are under constant scrutiny from our kids. It's time to rethink the kind of home you want for your ADHD kid and how you want to influence your children.

If you want nutrition and health to be a priority for your kids, it has to be one for you as well. Want your kids to go to church or volunteer with local non-profits? Start making phone calls and find where you can help. And any parent who wants their kids to study and get good grades needs to be open to reading more, spending time in extended education classes, and sharing what they learn with their kids.

Remember, all the copying and close observation from your kids is a good thing! It can push you to work harder, try new things, build good habits, and push yourself. Let your kids see you stumble and get yourself back up. It will show them they can do it, too.

You're the Model - Set a Positive Example

I'm always surprised to hear how parents talk about their kids versus how kids talk about their parents. One client, Susan, told me she had no respect for her mother.

"That surprises me," I told her. "I respect your mother. She works hard, always looks lovely, and spends her holidays volunteering."

Susan burst into tears and went red. She balled up her fists and yelled, "But she can't apologize when she shrinks my favorite blouse!"

That session was eye-opening for me. It reminded me how kids notice every little thing we do, and just because something seems inconsequential, like a shrunken blouse, they have a significant impact. Susan planned to wear a special outfit to a party but had to settle for her everyday look after her mother's mistake. She explained why she was angry using techniques I'd taught her to control her emotions, but it didn't get her the "I'm sorry" she deserved.

The experience taught her all the wrong lessons. Instead of learning that clothes aren't so important, she internalized her mother's lack of respect for others and began to copy it.

Even though they are important, we have to do more than eat healthily or go to the gym. We need to let our kids see our mistakes, hear us say that we're sorry, and then understand that forgiving ourselves and others is better than holding a grudge.

Here are some other ways you can set a positive example for your kids:

- Be vulnerable - don't emphasize a brave face, but rather open up about your pain, frustration, and sorrow in a way that starts a dialogue. When you share your trials, your kids will also come to you with their struggles.
- Practice gratitude - use family drives or meal times as a chance to discuss what's going well in your life and how you feel about it. Encourage your kids, partner, and friends to reflect on positive things happening for them as well.
- Be hospitable - Invite friends and neighbors over for game nights or meals. Ask them to help you plan snacks, what games to play, or how the night should go. Show your kids how great it is

to have people in your life, the value of friendship, and the art of being a good host.
- Celebrate your successes and your child's progress - one of the best lessons we can teach our kids is to stop and smell the roses when something goes well. Maybe we didn't make a million dollars or become movie stars, but we worked hard and achieved a goal. That's worth a special banana split or a weekend trip.
- Develop a passion for life - show your kids that life is fun and exciting. This might require some searching, but look for something that lights you up. It might be a new group of friends, a new skill, or some self-exploration. Whatever it is, share with your child how excited you are and let them see your enthusiasm.

When Your Child is Hypersensitive to Energies

Some children fall into the category of being an empath or an extremely sensitive person. If you notice your child often avoids big groups, is prone to headaches or stomach aches, and just seems to always know when a person is hiding something or feeling off, you may have an empath on your hands.

Many empathetic children get written off by those around them as too "shy" or "emotional" because, well, they feel a lot! The empaths I know often burst into tears, feel pain in their bodies when others are injured, or feel crushed at the sight of a homeless person or accident victim. It's beautiful to have someone in our lives who reminds us to think of others, but it also requires a different approach in our parenting.

Here are four common signs your child is an empath:

1. She's extra sensitive to emotional and physical stimulation. Sad movies leave her in tears, and T-shirt tags bother her all day.
2. She loves time alone. Many empaths have imaginary friends as children who they vastly prefer to physical humans. She may also struggle to play in group activities.
3. She gets struck hard by displays of cruelty. Even if she just sees a bully hurting someone else, it's too much for her.
4. She needs quite a while to calm down. A long school day can leave her drained, she loves to take naps, and she appreciates cuddle time with the family pet. Empaths struggle to maintain energy in highly social situations and do better in one-on-one settings.

When it comes to parenting an empath, you can do a few things to be supportive and understanding. Yes, your child will cry more and struggle at the sight of the world's injustices, but that doesn't mean she has to suffer day in and day out.

Start with stress management. Teach her how to do deep breathing exercises, meditate, anything that might help her keep her distress and anxiety down. Also, do a check on your stress level. Are you calm? If not, she'll feel it.

Help her say no to requests. Empaths have such big hearts they struggle to prioritize themselves. Talk about the importance of setting boundaries and how we know we have good friends when they respect our time and our wishes.

Keep her schedule light and allow for some unstructured time, but also remember that loud, crowded spaces will be a struggle. Ask if there is any quiet space you might use to help her calm down or just hug her before trying again. Talk to parents before you go to any big social gatherings for kids and let them know you may need to duck out without warning.

Talk about her empathetic state as a gift, not something she needs to change. Teach her all about what it means to be an empath and tell her how lucky she is, that she can feel what others feel, understand why people do certain things, and how only one to two percent of people are like her. Help her celebrate her incredible ability, don't try to change it.

Your Child's Mind is a Sponge

No matter your child's personality type, it will require a strong foundation. Your child's first six years of life build a kind of foundation that the rest of his life will use to create a mental landscape. Early stimulation, interactions with TV, caretakers, and parents all decide what kind of adult he will become.

Think of it this way - a child can absorb a whole new behavior after watching 20 seconds of television. Imagine what he can learn in an hour! You need to monitor what your child watches and for how long. Ideally, you want to watch it with him, but if you can't, you need to decide ahead of time what's okay and what's not okay for him to see.

If your child is still in these early stages, take advantage. Answer as many of his questions as you can, and if you don't know something, say, "I'm not sure, let's look it up," and then head to the library. Let your child see you reading, learning something new, eating green food, anything you want to impress on him as important. And, of course, laugh and play together whenever you can and show him how life can be fun!

Your child's older years are equally important, but you need to remember that any early trauma will continue to affect your child throughout his life. He'll also struggle to develop any habits he might not have picked up early. This is where a good life coach, an open dialogue, and good teachers can help. Acknowledge what happened (or didn't happen), and use it as a starting point. All the kids and teens I know really appreciate it when the adults in their lives are honest with them about the reality of a situation and how they plan to move forward.

Helping Your Child Thrive

Kids are so much smarter than we think, and I see the evidence all around me. When parents stop and really observe their kids, talk to them and, most importantly, listen attentively, they realize it too. You want to do more than get your kids through the day - you want them to thrive! Kids with the right mental state, a good attitude, and a solid support system can tackle anything and feel more optimistic about their future.

I've seen some consistent traits in parents who help their kids thrive instead of just surviving. Here are some habits I recommend you build up:

- Teach your kids to be aware of their thinking patterns. If your child is constantly judging himself for not looking, acting, or fitting in, he'll never give himself a break. Teach him to reframe negative thoughts so he can benefit, not suffer.
- Balance activities with downtime. Teach your children the beauty of relaxation and then practice it.
- Celebrate all the little things. Go out and look at the sunset, follow the moon's phases, or observe the plants in your neighborhood or garden. Kids who appreciate the little things

feel more grateful for what they have in their lives.
- Practice problem solving and talk openly about what changes your family needs to make. Are you all a messy bunch? Discuss what habits might help your household become more organized. Show your child how to tackle a problem, not avoid it.
- Have a vision. Many of us lose sight of our dream for ourselves as we enter the rat race and start paying bills, but it's different for kids. Take advantage and encourage them to visualize the kind of adult they want to be - selfless, musical, inventive? What gets them excited? Help them find other adults who can model that lifestyle for them to decide if it's the right choice.

They're A LOT Smarter Than You Think

Before I end this chapter, I want to discuss an odd phenomenon that happens in most cases of ADHD.

Surprisingly, most kids with ADHD test exceptionally high on IQ tests. However, that high score coincides with a difficulty performing simple functions. What does that mean for you as a parent? It means your child will give 100 percent of her time and attention to something she truly loves. But, you'll have to help her with everything else.

So, find ways to celebrate that unique genius and accept that she won't be able to maintain a to-do list without help or work through a task without a timer. That's why you and your family are there - to help her with the little stuff so she can dig deep into the big things that she loves.

Rather than try to change our ADHD kids, it's up to us to support them and show them what makes them so unique. I hope this book helped you see that and made you feel confident you can move forward as a knowledgeable, loving parent who understands this particular mental state on a deeper level.

Don't stop here! Keep doing the research, reading, and learning how to be the best parent you can be and all the ins and outs of ADHD. Remember, the more you know about it, the better you can help your child understand her mental state. That's the best gift you can give her.

Chapter Summary

- As parents, we need to work on ourselves to help our kids develop their best selves.
- Let your child see you eat well, exercise, read, and learn new things.
- Being vulnerable, grateful, and hospitable are simple things you can do to help your child develop a loving personality.

FINAL WORDS

Facing ADHD, really giving it a hard look, and accepting it into our lives as a family can be terrifying. Yet, something incredible happens when we go for it and accept this kind of brain as different, not wrong, or a lost cause. Our ADHD kids start to flourish. Maybe not in the way we expected, perhaps they'll never be what we pictured back when they were babies, but they will be something better - their authentic selves.

I know I wrote a lot about diet changes, a steady sleep schedule, and plenty of exercise as a way of helping your child, but please don't discredit medication. Most kids who work with doctors eventually find a dosage that works for them and helps them be less impulsive. Remember that impulsivity can lead to many dangerous behaviors as kids get older, like reckless driving, drinking, or taking more risks than average.

Starting meds at a young age can be a big boost for an ADHD kid, but it won't ever be a savior. Kids who have orderly, structured homes that focus on health and cleanliness do significantly better. They respond to that proactive nature, and parents feel better when they prepare for meltdowns or problems ahead of time. Even reading up on ADHD is a big step in the right direction.

I hope you use this book as inspiration to not just care for your kid but also to take control of your health, both mentally and emotionally. Raising kids with ADHD is a unique challenge and one that will demand all your strength and energy. Replenish! It's important. Remember, once parents put a premium on their mental health and stability, kids start to respect it as well.

I also hope this book makes you rethink how you interact with your family. Do you let yourself be vulnerable, or do you put on a brave face no matter what? Are you open about what you're learning, or do you dismiss this idea of continuing your education? Adopting a new attitude about sharing our lives with our children can shift our family dynamic in a big way. Telling our kids the truth no matter what, sharing our hardships, and celebrating our successes with them can bond us all together and create something beautiful.

Writing this book was an incredible experience, and I hope you enjoyed reading it as much as I did putting it together. I love to work with kids and parents, and this project let me do that in a new way that I truly enjoyed!

FINAL WORDS

Thank you for giving me your precious time. If you enjoyed this book, please leave me a comment and a star rating on Amazon or Audible! Your reviews help others find this book. I hope you'll check out my other books, all of which are available online.

PLEASE REVIEW MY BOOK YOU CAN MAKE A DIFFERENCE

Enjoy this book? You can make a huge difference!

Reviews are the most powerful tool for authors when it comes to getting attention for our books! As much as I would love to have tons of money to throw at advertising I'm simply not there yet.

However... loyal readers such as yourself can make all the difference. Honest reviews of my book help bring them to the attention of other readers.

If you enjoyed my book I would be grateful if you would spend just five minutes leaving a review (as short or as long as you want it to be!) You can do so by simply clicking on the following link or typing it into your web browser.

https://www.amazon.com/review/create-review/?asin=B09W4HMSTJ

Thank you so much for your time!

ABOUT THE AUTHOR

Elizabeth N. Jacobs resides in Iowa with her husband, six year-old son and two dogs. She stays very busy between family life and running her own business. Elizabeth has always had a passion for children and a listening ear for those needing a confidant. This is Elizabeth's second book, though she has plans for several more all diving deeper into children, marriage and relationships.

For more information: Elizabeth@elizabethnjacobs.com

OTHER BOOKS BY ELIZABETH N. JACOBS

REFERENCES

"5 Ways to Help Your Children Express Themselves | Sunshine House." Sunshine House Early Learning Academy, sunshinehouse.com/blog/5-ways-to-help-your-children-express-themselves. Accessed 20 Oct. 2021.

"7 Keys to Helping Kids Set and Achieve Goals." Verywell Family, 22 June 2020, www.verywellfamily.com/helping-kids-set-and-achieve-goals-4121002.

"7 Tips for Effective Communication with Your School-Aged Child - Child Development and Parenting: Middle Childhood." Mental Help, www.mentalhelp.net/blogs/7-tips-for-effective-communication-with-your-school-aged-child. Accessed 20 Oct. 2021.

"10 Tips For Coping With A Hyperactive Child." EverydayHealth.Com, 15 Nov. 2017, www.everydayhealth.

com/emotional-health/adhd/10-tips-coping-with-hyperactive-child.

"10 Tips for Limiting Your Child's Screen Time." Verywell Family, 17 Sept. 2020, www.verywellfamily.com/tips-for-limiting-electronics-and-screen-time-for-kids-1094870.ADDitude Editors.

"Take a Deep Breath: Teaching Kids to Control Emotions." ADDitude, 25 June 2021, www.additudemag.com/emotional-control-for-kids.---.

"The Neuroscience of the ADHD Brain." ADDitude, 10 May 2021, www.additudemag.com/neuroscience-of-adhd-brain.ADDitude Editors, and ADDitude's Adhd Medical Review Panel.

"ADHD Coping Strategies You Haven't Tried Yet." ADDitude, 9 July 2021, www.additudemag.com/dealing-with-adhd-80-coping-strategies.Admin.

"5 Ways to Help Children Identify and Express Their Emotions." MindChamps, 17 June 2020, www.mindchamps.org/blog/help-children-identify-express-emotions.All4Kids.

"Creating a Safe & Open Home Environment." Child Abuse Prevention, Treatment & Welfare Services | Children's Bureau, 19 Mar. 2021, www.all4kids.org/news/blog/creating-a-safe-open-home-environment.

"Anxiety and Fear in Children - Better Health Channel." Better Health, www.betterhealth.vic.gov.au/health/conditionsandtreatments/fear-and-anxiety-children. Accessed 20 Oct. 2021

."Attention-Deficit/Hyperactivity Disorder (ADHD) in Children - Symptoms and Causes." Mayo Clinic, 25 June 2019, www.mayoclinic.org/diseases-conditions/adhd/symptoms-causes/syc-20350889.Austin, Daryl.

"6 Reasons Why Yelling at Kids Doesn't Actually Work." Parents, 7 May 2021, www.parents.com/health/healthy-happy-kids/a-parental-wake-up-call-yelling-doesnt-help.Battles, Magdalena.

"Are You Taking The Leash Off And Letting Your Child Be Free To Play?" Lifehack, 27 Feb. 2018, www.lifehack.org/640696/the-most-difficult-lesson-for-parents-let-children-play.

"Beyond Inattention: How ADHD May Be Affecting Your Life." WebMD, www.webmd.com/add-adhd/ss/slideshow-adhd-life. Accessed 20 Oct. 2021.Bhatnagar, Ekta Sharma, and Ekta Sharma Bhatnagar.

"7 Effective Games & Activities To Handle Hyperactive Kids." Flintobox, 7 May 2020, flintobox.com/blog/parenting/handle-hyperactive-kids.Braaten, Ellen, PhD.

"ADHD Medication for Kids: Is It Safe? Does It Help?" Harvard Health, 4 Mar. 2016, www.health.harvard.edu/blog/adhd-medication-for-kids-is-it-safe-does-it-help-201603049235.Bregel, Sarah.

REFERENCES

"Why I Don't Force My Kids To Do Stuff." Fatherly, 26 Aug. 2020, www.fatherly.com/play/dont-force-kids-hobbies-dont-like.Burns, Julie R.

"How to Get Kids to Eat Vegetables and Healthy Foods." Parents, 15 June 2021, www.parents.com/kids/nutrition/healthy-eating/get-your-kids-to-eat-better.

"Calm Yourself, Then Teach." AHA Parenting, www.aha-parenting.com/read/When-Your-Child-Makes-You-Want-To-Scream. Accessed 20 Oct. 2021.

"Can You Treat ADHD Without Drugs?" WebMD, 4 Aug. 2015, www.webmd.com/add-adhd/childhood-adhd/can-you-treat-adhd-without-drugs.Carrie Shrier, Michigan State University Extension.

"Young Children Learn by Copying You!" MSU Extension, 17 Mar. 2021, www.canr.msu.edu/news/young_children_learn_by_copying_you.Casano, Tom.

"The Power of Aligning Your Life with Your Truth." Life Coach Spotter, 22 Feb. 2021, www.lifecoachspotter.com/aligning-your-life-with-your-truth.Cherney, Kristeen.

"Why 'Being Smart' Doesn't Help People with ADHD." Healthline, 1 Mar. 2019, www.healthline.com/health/adhd/iq-adhd.Child Mind Institute.

"Helping Young Children Who Are Socially Anxious." Child Mind Institute, 25 Aug. 2021, childmind.org/article/how-to-help-anxious-kids-in-social-situations.---.

"How to Help Children Manage Fears." Child Mind Institute, 16 Aug. 2021, childmind.org/article/help-children-manage-fears.---.

"Hyperfocus: The Flip Side of ADHD?" Child Mind Institute, 19 Aug. 2021, childmind.org/article/hyperfocus-the-flip-side-of-adhd.Childventures.

"Reasons Why Patience Is Important In Childcare." Childventures, 19 Aug. 2017, childventures.ca/blog/2016/11/reasons-patience-important-childcare.

"Communicating Well with Babies and Children: Tips." Raising Children Network, 31 Aug. 2020, raisingchildren.net.au/toddlers/connecting-communicating/communicating/communicating-well-with-children.

"Core Beliefs and Self Acceptance." Better Relationships, www.betterrelationships.org.au/well-being/core-beliefs-self-acceptance. Accessed 20 Oct. 2021.Cultivate, Create &Amp;

"How to Overcome Limiting Beliefs, According to a Career and Life Coach." Create & Cultivate, 20 Aug. 2020, www.createcultivate.com/blog/how-to-overcome-limiting-beliefs.Dacher, Elliott.

"7 Steps to Overcoming the Overactive Mind." HuffPost, 26 Apr. 2017, www.huffpost.com/entry/7-steps-to-overcoming-the_b_9771442.Dad, All Pro.

"10 Ways to Make Your Child Feel Secure." All Pro Dad, 20 July 2021, www.allprodad.com/10-ways-to-make-your-child-feel-secure.

"Default - Stanford Children's Health." Stanford Children, www.stanfordchildrens.org/en/topic/default?id=letting-kids-grow-upat-their-own-pace-1-585. Accessed 20 Oct. 2021.Elgan, Mike.

"Smartphones Make People Distracted and Unproductive." Computerworld, 12 Aug. 2017, www.computerworld.com/article/3215276/smartphones-make-people-distracted-and-unproductive.html#:%7E:text=The%20more%20dependent%20people%20are,sound%20of%20our%20own%20names.&text=Distracted%20workers%20are%20unproductive.Evitt, Marie Faust.

"7 Tips for Teaching Kids How to Set Goals (And Reach Them!)." Parents, 14 Nov. 2019, www.parents.com/parenting/better-parenting/style/how-to-teach-kids-perseverance-goal-setting.Flanagan, Patricia. "The Best Way to Help When Your Child 'Just Doesn't Fit In.' Understood, 22 Oct. 2020, www.understood.org/articles/en/the-best-way-to-help-when-your-child-just-doesnt-fit-in.Foley, Miriam.

"6 Best Ways to Manage Your Child's Anger." Parents, 19 May 2021, www.parents.com/toddlers-preschoolers/discipline/anger-management/anger-managment-in-children-best-ways-to-help-kids.Goldberg, Susan.

"When Your Child Has a Very Bad Temper." Today's Parent, 10 Feb. 2017, www.todaysparent.com/kids/when-your-child-has-a-very-bad-temper.Gross, Gail.

"Parenting With Patience." HuffPost, 5 Mar. 2017, www.huffpost.com/entry/parenting-with-patience_b_9380880.

"Growth and Development: Helping Your Child Build Self-Esteem | CS Mott Children's Hospital | Michigan Medicine." Mott Children, www.mottchildren.org/health-library/tk1326. Accessed 20 Oct. 2021.Harding, Sharon.

"How To Accept Your Children Just As They Are." Rediscovered Families, 25 Aug. 2016, rediscoveredfamilies.com/learning-to-accept-your-children.Harpin, V.

"The Effect of ADHD on the Life of an Individual, Their Family, and Community from Preschool to Adult Life." Archives of Disease in Childhood, 1 Feb. 2005, adc.bmj.com/content/90/suppl_1/i2.Haykal, Muhammad.

"Family Support is The Most Significant Factor in People Success - Kompasiana.com." KOMPASIANA, 18 June 2015, www.kompasiana.com/muhammadhaykal/54f6b5e7a33311ea5a8b478c/family-support-is-the-most-significant-factor-in-people-success.

"Help! What to Do When My Child Has a Meltdown." Attuned Psychology, 20 Apr. 2018, attunedpsychology.com/help-what-to-do-when-my-child-has-a-meltdown.

"Helping Children Communicate | Scholastic." Scholastic, www.scholastic.com/teachers/articles/teaching-content/helping-children-communicate. Accessed 20 Oct. 2021.Henze, Rachel.

"Empower Children with ADHD and Let Them Thrive •." Learning Links, 15 Sept. 2020, www.learninglinks.org.au/empower-children-with-adhd.Hill, Laura Wheatman.

"4 Signs Your Child Is an Empath—and How to Parent an Emotionally or Physically Sensitive Child." Parents, 15 Apr. 2021, www.parents.com/kids/health/signs-your-child-is-an-empathand-how-to-parent-an-emotionally-or-physically-sensitive-child.Hill, Tamara.

"6 Things Kids Need From Adults to Feel Valued." PsychAlive, 2 Nov. 2013, www.psychalive.org/6-things-kids-need-from-adults-to-feel-valued.Hjalmarsdottir, Freydis M.

"Does Nutrition Play a Role in ADHD?" Healthline, 30 Jan. 2020, www.healthline.com/nutrition/nutrition-and-adhd.

"How Forced Schooling Harms Children." Alternatives to School, 10 Sept. 2014, alternativestoschool.com/articles/how-school-wounds.

"How the ADHD Brain Biologically Differs From the Non-ADHD Brain." Verywell Mind, 5 Jan. 2021, www.verywellmind.com/the-adhd-brain-4129396.

"How to Better Understand Your Child." Greater Good, greatergood.berkeley.edu/article/item/how_to_better_understand_your_child. Accessed 20 Oct. 2021.

"How to Empower Children to Take Charge of Their Own Learning." The New Age Parents, thenewageparents.com/how-to-empower-children-to-take-charge-of-their-own-learning. Accessed 20 Oct. 2021.

"How to Help a Highly Emotional Child Cope With Big Feelings." Verywell Family, 22 Mar. 2021, www.verywellfamily.com/how-to-help-an-overly-emotional-child-4157594.Hunter, Elaine.

"'Children Are like Little Sponges': Early Learning Can Set Them up for Life." Theirworld, 18 Jan. 2018, theirworld.org/news/early-learning-sets-up-young-children-for-life.Jepsen, Deborah.

"10 Ways You Can Teach Your Child How to Thrive." Melbourne Child Psychology & School Psychology Services, 16 Aug. 2013, www.melbournechildpsychology.com.au/blog/10-ways-you-can-teach-your-child-how-to-thrive.

"Just How Effective Are ADHD Meds?" WebMD, 23 July 2019, www.webmd.com/add-adhd/childhood-adhd/news/20190723/just-how-effective-are-adhd-meds.Kazda, Luise Mph.

"Overdiagnosis of Attention-Deficit/Hyperactivity Disorder in Children and Adolescents: A Systematic Scoping." Jama Network, 12 Apr. 2021, jamanetwork.com/journals/jamanetworkopen/fullarticle/2778451.Kessler, Zoë.

"The Secret to No-Shout, No-Tears Discipline." ADDitude, 20 July 2021, www.additudemag.com/discipline-without-yelling-calm-parenting-for-kids-with-adhd.

"Kids and Food: 10 Tips for Parents (for Parents) - Nemours Kidshealth." Kids Health, kidshealth.org/en/parents/eating-tips.html. Accessed 20 Oct. 2021.Koerth-Baker, Maggie.

"The Not-So-Hidden Cause Behind the A.D.H.D. Epidemic." The New York Times, 3 Nov. 2013, www.nytimes.com/2013/10/20/magazine/the-not-so-hidden-cause-behind-the-adhd-epidemic.html.Lehman, James Msw, and James Msw Lehman.

"What to Do When Children Don't Fit In." Empowering Parents, 17 May 2021, www.empoweringparents.com/article/when-your-child-says-i-dont-fit-in.Lehman, Janet Msw, and Janet Msw Lehman.

"Parent the Child You Have, Not the Child You Wish You Had." Empowering Parents, 17 May 2021, www.empoweringparents.com/article/parent-child-you-have.Lerner, Claire.

"Understanding and Supporting Highly Sensitive (HS) Children." Child Development and Parent Consultation, 13 Sept. 2021, www.lernerchilddevelopment.com/mainblog/2018/7/25/ddnt-ever-say-that-to-me-again-do-you-understand-do-you-understand-how-to-respond-to-highly-sensitive-reactive-children.

"Let Your Child Be on Their Own Time Line | National Association for Gifted Children." National Association for Gifted Children, www.nagc.org/blog/let-your-child-be-their-own-time-line. Accessed 20 Oct. 2021.Lewison, Kiera.

"10 Ways How to Overcome Challenges Life Throws at You." University of the People, 7 Jan. 2021, www.uopeople.edu/blog/10-ways-how-to-overcome-challenges.-Lynch, Laura.

"7 Major Learning Styles and the 1 Big Mistake Everyone Makes." LearnDash, 14 Jan. 2020, www.learndash.com/7-major-learning-styles-which-one-is-you.Mancall-Bitel, Nicholas.

"How Can a Distracted Generation Learn Anything?" BBC Worklife, www.bbc.com/worklife/article/20190220-how-can-a-distracted-generation-learn-anything. Accessed 20 Oct. 2021.McCabe, Jessica.

"A Day In the Life with ADHD: The Ups and Downs." Healthline, 18 Apr. 2019, www.healthline.com/health/adhd/adult-adhd/a-day-in-the-life.McDonald, Trevor.

"5 Ways to Set a Good Example for Your Kids." The Good Men Project, 6 Dec. 2017, goodmenproject.com/featured-content/5-ways-set-good-example-kids-lbkr.Melinda.

"ADHD Parenting Tips." HelpGuide.Org, 21 Sept. 2021, www.helpguide.org/articles/add-adhd/when-your-child-has-attention-deficit-disorder-adhd.htm.Melissa.

"How to Help Your Child Set SMART Goals to Focus & Achieve." Ninja Focus, 7 Jan. 2020, www.ninjafocus.com/how-to-help-your-child-set-goals.Miniapple2.

"5 Benefits Of Encouraging Your Child To Pursue All Of Their Passions." Miniapple International Montessori, 13 June 2019, miniapplemontessori.com/5-benefits-encouraging-child-pursue-passions.

"NewsGP - Research Finds ADHD Is Overdiagnosed, but Experts Remain Unconvinced." NewsGP, www1.racgp.org.au/newsgp/clinical/research-finds-adhd-is-overdiagnosed-but-experts-r. Accessed 20 Oct. 2021.NHS website.

"Symptoms." Nhs.Uk, 21 Sept. 2020, www.nhs.uk/conditions/attention-deficit-hyperactivity-disorder-adhd/symptoms.---. "Treatment." Nhs.Uk, 25 Mar. 2021, www.nhs.uk/conditions/attention-deficit-hyperactivity-disorder-adhd/treatment.Norman, Rachel.

"Why Kids Need To Fit In Before They Can Be Themselves." A Mother Far from Home, 1 Aug. 2021, amotherfarfromhome.com/help-your-child-socialize.Norris, Emma.

"A Psychologist on 5 Ways to Calm an Overactive Mind before Bed." Ladders | Business News & Career Advice, 14 Oct. 2019, www.theladders.com/career-advice/a-psychologist-on-5-ways-to-calm-an-overactive-mind-before-bed.

"Now What? A Step-by-Step Guide for When Your Child Is Diagnosed With ADHD." WebMD, 20 June 2018, www.webmd.com/add-adhd/childhood-adhd/child-adhd-diagnosis-guide.

"The Obstacle Is the Way by Ryan Holiday." YouTube, 24 Oct. 2015, www.youtube.com/watch?v=2rQfr7X-AQi0.Oglethorpe, Martine.

"Why Being a Kid Today Is Hard." Momtastic, 1 Nov. 2016, www.momtastic.com/parenting/655725-kid-today-hard.Orenstein, Beth, and Pat F. Bass III MD.

"8 Steps to Stop Your Child From Having an ADHD Meltdown." EverydayHealth.Com, 10 Nov. 2014, www.everydayhealth.com/add-adhd/8-steps-to-stop-your-child-from-having-an-adhd-meltdown.aspx.Orson, Kate.

"10 Reasons Your Toddler's Tantrum Is Actually a Good Thing." Parents, 9 Oct. 2019, www.parents.com/toddlers-preschoolers/discipline/tantrum/10-reasons-your-toddlers-tantrum-is-actually-a-good-thing.Outlook, New Life.

"7 Ways to Calm Your Child with ADHD." Healthline, 26 Mar. 2018, www.healthline.com/health/adhd/calm-children-natural-remedies.Pandey, Kajal.

"11 Ways to Improve Your Relationship With Yourself." HuffPost, 4 June 2017, www.huffpost.com/entry/11-ways-to-improve-your-r_b_10269696.Paradigmtreat.

"Teens Need to Feel Loved and Accepted." Paradigm Treatment, 14 Aug. 2021, paradigmtreatment.com/teens-need-to-feel-loved-and-accepted.Pincus, Debbie Lmhc, and Debbie Lmhc Pincus.

"How to Control Your Anger with Kids." Empowering Parents, 5 Oct. 2021, www.empoweringparents.com/article/calm-parenting-get-control-child-making-angry.-Porter, Eloise.

"Parenting Tips for ADHD: Do's and Don'ts." Healthline, 17 Sept. 2018, www.healthline.com/health/adhd/parenting-tips.Post, Guest.

"5 Ways To Turn Your Child's Hyperactivity Into Productivity - Friendship Circle - Special Needs Blog." Friendship Circle -- Special Needs Blog, 15 Nov. 2013, www.friendshipcircle.org/blog/2012/10/26/5-ways-to-turn-your-childs-hyperactivity-to-productivity

"Reasons Why It Is so Important to Encourage Independence In Children." Schoolhouse Day Care, 16 Jan. 2020, schoolhouse-daycare.co.uk/blog/why-you-should-encourage-independence.Reinke, Darren.

"The Enemy Within: How to Overcome Self-Limiting Beliefs." Group Sixty, 3 Feb. 2021, www.groupsixty.com/ideas-blog/2021/1/27/the-enemy-within-how-to-overcome-self-limiting-beliefs.

"Relaxation Is a Skill; Why Our Kids Need It and How to Make It a Regular Practice in Their Life." WELLBEAN, www.wellbean.us/blog/relaxation-why-our-children-need-it-and-10-ways-to-practice. Accessed 20 Oct. 2021.Richardson, Helen.

'No One Loves Me': Changing a Child's Belief System from the Inside Out." Focus on the Family, 11 Dec. 2020, www.focusonthefamily.com/pro-life/foster-care/no-one-loves-me-changing-a-childs-belief-system-from-the-inside-out.Rosen, Peg.

"ADHD and Boredom." Understood, 2 Apr. 2021, www.understood.org/articles/en/adhd-and-boredom-what-you-need-to-know.Rucklidge, Julia J., PhD, et al.

"Do Diet and Nutrition Affect ADHD? Facts and Clinical Considerations." Psychiatric Times, 16 Nov. 2020, www.psychiatrictimes.com/view/do-diet-and-nutrition-affect-adhd-facts-and-clinical-considerations.Russell, Lucy.

"When Your Child Doesn't Fit In." They Are the Future, 30 Sept. 2021, www.theyarethefuture.co.uk/when-child-doesnt-fit-in.

"Self-Esteem in Children: 1–8 Years." Raising Children Network, 7 May 2021, raisingchildren.net.au/toddlers/behaviour/understanding-behaviour/about-self-esteem#primary-school-age-children-and-self-esteem-nav-title.Shea, Molly.

"15 Easy Ways to Set a Good Example for Your Kid." Parents, 31 May 2019, www.parents.com/parenting/better-parenting/positive/easy-ways-to-set-a-good-example-for-your-kid.Siner, Kate.

"Why You Should Learn Your Personal Truth." Dr Kate Siner, 28 Dec. 2019, katesiner.com/learn-personal-truth.Staff, GreatSchools.

"6 Ways to Help Your Child Deal with Peer Pressure." Parenting, 5 Sept. 2019, www.greatschools.org/gk/articles/6-tips-resisting-peer-pressure.Staff, Parenting Today.

"Child Psychology and Mental Health." Child Development Institute, 23 July 2019, childdevelopmentinfo.com/child-psychology.Standen, Casey.

"How to Empower Kids to Own Their Learning." Cluey Learning, 14 Oct. 2020, clueylearning.com.au/blog/how-to-empower-kids-to-own-their-learning.State, Clearinghouse For Military Family Readiness At Penn.

"Talking to Children About Peer Pressure – Thrive." PSU, thrive.psu.edu/blog/talking-to-children-about-peer-pressure. Accessed 20 Oct. 2021.Stiefel, Chana.

"What Your Child Learns By Imitating You." Parents, 5 Oct. 2005, www.parents.com/toddlers-preschoolers/development/behavioral/what-your-child-learns-by-imitating-you.Storebø, Ole Jakob.

"Methylphenidate for Attention-Deficit/Hyperactivity Disorder in Children and Adolescents: Cochrane Systematic Review with Meta-Analyses and Trial Sequential Analyses of Randomised Clinical Trials." The BMJ, 25 Nov. 2015, www.bmj.com/content/351/bmj.h5203.Summersault, Anastasia.

"Stop Forcing Your Kids On A Path To Conformity - Age of Awareness." Medium, 28 Oct. 2020, medium.com/age-of-awareness/stop-forcing-your-kids-on-a-path-to-conformity-b68c800d87c2.

"Taming Tempers (for Parents) - Nemours Kidshealth." Kids Health, kidshealth.org/en/parents/temper.html. Accessed 20 Oct. 2021.

"Tantrums: Why They Happen and How to Respond." Raising Children Network, 18 May 2020, raisingchildren.net.au/toddlers/behaviour/crying-tantrums/tantrums.Taylor, Jen.

"The Empathetic Child - Jennifer Taylor Play Therapy." Jen Taylor Play Therapy, 20 Feb. 2018, jentaylorplaytherapy.com/empathetic-child.the Healthline Editorial Team.

"14 Signs of Attention Deficit Hyperactivity Disorder (ADHD)." Healthline, 19 Feb. 2020, www.healthline.com/health/adhd/signs.Thomas, Liji, MD. "How Does ADHD Affect the Brain?" News-Medical.Net, 26 Feb. 2019, www.news-medical.net/health/How-does-ADHD-Affect-the-Brain.aspx.

"Tips to Help Kids Embrace Their Uniqueness and Practice Self-Love." PBS SoCal, 8 July 2021, www.pbssocal.org/education/tips-help-kids-embrace-uniqueness-practice-self-love.Todd, Carolyn.

"Why Are So Many More Children Being Diagnosed With ADHD Today?" SELF, 24 Sept. 2018, www.self.-

com/story/adhd-diagnosis-rates-children-increase. Tugend, Alina.

"9 Secrets of Confident Kids." Parents, 11 June 2015, www.parents.com/toddlers-preschoolers/development/fear/secrets-of-confident-kids. Vasudev, Meera, and Meera Vasudev.

"18 Essential Life Skills To Equip Your Child For The Real World." Flintobox, 11 May 2020, flintobox.com/blog/child-development/life-skills.

"Ways to Encourage and Celebrate Your Child's Uniqueness." Verywell Family, 14 July 2020, www.verywellfamily.com/celebrate-childs-uniqueness-5071090.

"We All Learn Differently, and That's OK." The Arizona State Press, 30 Mar. 2017, www.statepress.com/article/2017/03/spopinion-learning-styles-are-helpful-to-individualized-learning. Welling, Robyn.

"3 Tips For Helping Children Embrace Their Unique Selves." ParentsTogether, 11 Nov. 2019, parents-together.org/3-tips-for-helping-children-embrace-their-unique-selves

."What Is ADHD?" Centers for Disease Control and Prevention, 26 Jan. 2021, www.cdc.gov/ncbddd/adhd/facts.html.

"What Is ADHD?" Web Starter Kit, www.psychiatry.org/patients-families/adhd/what-is-adhd. Accessed 20 Oct. 2021.

"Why Your Childâs Brain Is like a Sponge." Age of Montessori, ageofmontessori.org/why-your-childs-brain-is-like-a-sponge. Accessed 20 Oct. 2021.Wiatrak, Brandi.

"20 Ways to Make Your Child Feel Loved and Valued." The Cultured Baby, 30 Sept. 2021, theculturedbaby.world/2019/06/14/ways-to-make-your-child-feel-loved-and-valued.Wong, Daniel.

"30 Simple Ways to Set a Good Example for Your Children." Daniel Wong, 30 Sept. 2021, www.daniel-wong.com/2019/08/26/set-good-example-for-your-children.Wright, Lexi Walters.

"5 'Unwritten' Social Rules That Some Kids Miss." Understood, 10 Mar. 2021, www.understood.org/articles/en/5-unwritten-social-rules.Yanklowitz, Shmuly.

"It's Hard to Be a Kid Today." HuffPost, 24 May 2014, www.huffpost.com/entry/its-hard-to-be-a-kid-today_b_5018406.ZERO TO THREE.

"How to Support Your Child's Communication Skills." ZERO TO THREE, www.zerotothree.org/resources/302-how-to-support-your-child-s-communication-skills. Accessed 20 Oct. 2021.Zivanovic, Vladimir.

"How to Create a Healthy and Safe Environment for Your Children." Lifehack, 24 Aug. 2016, www.lifehack.org/450968/how-to-create-a-healthy-and-safe-environment-for-your-children.